Scripture and Cosmos Reconciled

John Dewey Stahl

Copyright © 2014 by John Dewey Stahl

Scripture and Cosmos Reconciled
by John Dewey Stahl

Printed in the United States of America

ISBN 9781628715347

All rights reserved solely by the author. The author guarantees all contents are original and do not infringe upon the legal rights of any other person or work. No part of this book may be reproduced in any form without the permission of the author. The views expressed in this book are not necessarily those of the publisher.

Unless otherwise indicated, Bible quotations are taken from the New International Version. Copyright © 1973, 1978, 1984 by International Bible Society, Zondervan Publishing House; and from the New Revised Standard Version. Copyright © 1989 by the National Council of Churches, Harper Collins Publishers; and from the King James Version. All released by PC StudyBible for Windows. Copyright © 1992-2002, Biblesoft, Inc. Also quotations are taken from Tanakh, The Holy Scripture, The Standard Jewish Bible. Copyright © 1988 by The Jewish Publication Society.

www.xulonpress.com

Contents

Preface and Dedication vii

Acknowledgments xi

Chapter 1 In the Beginning Was the Word 13

Chapter 2 In the Beginning God Created 29

Chapter 3 Functions of Time, Weather, and Food 48

Chapter 4 Functionaries Installed 70

Chapter 5 Let Us Make Humans in Our Image 86

Chapter 6 God Blessed the Seventh Day as Holy: 93

Chapter 7 God, Adam and Eve in Relationship 100

Chapter 8 Adam and Eve Sin 135

Chapter 9 Some Perspectives 166

Chapter 10 Scripture and Cosmos Reconciled 180

Miscellaneous 195

    Time of Creation in Science and Scriptures
    Christian Hope: In My Father's House Are Many
    Mansions

Bibliography 199

End Notes 205

Preface and Dedication

I love science. I love the God who created everything scientists discover. I appreciate the Bible, including Genesis, as the inspired Word of God. But I also know something about the literary, cultural and organizational role of human authors, editors, redactors and translators in preparing the scriptural texts we have today. This topic is important to me personally. How does my faith experience relate to scientific knowledge? Personally, I value both.

I am intrigued by the role that oral tradition played in preserving the stories we now read in Genesis. Scholarship regarding this role is speculative and tentative. Having studied science at the graduate level, and teaching college chemistry and geology, I have a great respect for science's contribution to our understanding and appreciation of nature.

To pit Scripture against science or to view faith and science as two unrelated realms of knowledge strike me as a misunderstanding and disservice to both. Theoretically, the Creator's word and God's world should be in harmony. Too many writings on the topics of science and scripture tend to lack balance or are simply too dated in their understanding of one area of study or the other. This is an issue I have wrestled with much of my life, and so I am willing to risk a cross-disciplinary approach to the reading of Genesis.

I want this book to make a balanced contribution to the understanding of the first three chapters of Genesis in relation to relevant knowledge of current science. I do not propose to make an in-depth interpretation of the Hebrew text. I do think that we can make use of some scholarly tools for a broad approach to interpretation of scripture. Perhaps my greatest contribution can be to young persons of faith who feel called to make their contribution in the sciences, but are afraid that scientific study may jeopardize their faith. I want to show the weaknesses of creation theory that are popular in some Christian circles and that scientific knowledge can be complementary to a faithful reading and interpretation of the Genesis chapters.

By elucidating a truly biblical theology of God and creation, I want to show that God's hidden hand in nature is magnified by science when illuminated by the Spirit of Christ in a faith experience. It is part of my ministry to make scripture relevant to life in our culture. Scripture can stand firm alongside scientific knowledge. I expect this approach to be controversial, but hope that it can be a basis for significant discussion.

The important question is how to read and understand the Bible in relation to apparent conflicts with scientific discoveries. The importance of our approach to reading and understanding is exemplified by the polarization and rancor generated between some conservative Christians, specifically regarding evolution, and those Christians or scientists who hold that the evidence from science is compelling, including evidence for evolution.

As a child, I remember planetarium lectures given by M. T. Brackbill, suggesting that the earth and universe are billions of years old. After studying geology with D. Ralph Hostetter, I came to appreciate the scientific evidence for the age of the earth and the concept of geological time periods. This study raised the issues of evolution of biological organisms and the relationship of very old hominid fossils to human beings.

About a decade later, I continued my study of geology at James Madison University. By that time, geology had undergone a paradigm shift due to evidence in plate tectonics, unifying many concepts

Preface and Dedication

formerly inexplicable as taught by my early mentor. In preparation for teaching I was required to defend my own faith positions in relation to my understanding of science. Many things in the scientific disciplines pointed to the evolution of living things, but the accounts of Adam's formation from "dust" and Eve's creation from Adam's rib in Genesis, as I understood it, seemed like an uncrossable theological barrier to the evolution of human beings.

Most of the Christian views I was exposed to were very anti-evolutionary. There are a variety of Christian views today that accept evolution, but the average person in the pew has ideas that can be in tension with those of many Christian teachers of science and even their seminary-trained pastors.

I chose the topic of science and scripture to stimulate rational discussion between polarized views. This book shows that Scripture can stand firm alongside scientific knowledge. I believe that someday most Christians will accept many of the conclusions I have written about.

I hope to contribute to a paradigm shift that in the future will have the same kind of acceptance that the heliocentric view of earth, rather than the geocentric view, now has. An informed and faithful view of scripture and a scientific view of the cosmos can be reconciled. God's revealed word should not be thrown out with the casting of the naturalistic die of science that reveals the Bible to be a human book. Nor should the compelling evidence of science be ignored by turning the Bible into a supernatural book of magic.

God's hidden heart is communicated in Scripture, and God's hidden hand is communicated in the cosmos. Both are known through a faith experience and relationship with God. This is the nature of what I have studied and I am willing to defend.

Scripture and Cosmos Reconciled

Dedication:

To my father Dewey Stahl and my mother Mary Brubaker Stahl

Acknowledgments

I am particularly aware of the early roots of my life in the communities of faith and of scholarship. First I want to recognize those who have joined the "great cloud of witnesses." I am thankful for the third President of the institution now known as Eastern Mennonite University (EMU), J. L. Stauffer, who instructed and baptized me into the church and encouraged my expression of faith as a young boy. Professor M. T. Brackbill introduced me to the stars and stimulated my scientific imagination through planetarium lectures, always with the reverence of faith. Professor D. Ralph Hostetter began college classes with prayer and challenged me to understand scientific thinking, whether I agreed with it or not. He was my mentor for college teaching. President J. R. Mumaw, the fourth President of EMU and my former pastor, employed me for my first college teaching position. Professor C. K. Lehman taught my first seminary level course in biblical theology and opened my mind to new perspectives for understanding the texts of Genesis. Professor J. C. Wenger provided an immersion into Anabaptist theology. Professor G. Irvin Lehman provided a tour of biblical archeology.

I am also thankful for a cloud of living witnesses. President Myron Augsburger, the fifth President of EMU, challenged me to make a Christian contribution in the larger academic context and employed me in teaching and administrative roles. In seminary studies I took after my first retirement, I received a warm and stimulating welcome by faculty. Dr. James Engle, my professor for many Old Testament classes, also served as adviser for my seminary thesis. I thank him and the rest of the committee of readers, Dr. Roman Miller, college Professor of Biology, Dr. Sarah Wenger Shenk, Associate Dean and Associate Professor of Christian Practices and now President of Anabaptist Mennonite Seminary, and Dr. Anil Solanki, Professor of Old Testament, for accepting the assignment to evaluate a cross-disciplinary thesis that could appear somewhat unusual. My seminary thesis is a primary basis for this book.

A special thank you to the editors that worked on this book: my wife – Susan L. Stahl, persons from Honest Editing and Writers Edge and especially Rachel K. Stahl for final work on the whole book.

Chapter 1

In the Beginning Was the Word

Some Starting Points for Looking at the Genesis Story of Creation

In looking at the creation story in Genesis, there are several things we should keep in mind:

First, an understanding of the culture of those who brought us the text of Genesis is basic for understanding its meaning.

Second, many cultural changes and new understandings of nature, especially the development of science, impact our reading of Genesis today. Much change and complexity has affected the text of Genesis from its possible inception as an oral account by the early ancestors to its present text in our printed Bibles.

Third, the development of the whole Bible, particularly the revelation of Jesus Christ, is the primary basis for developing theology. Knowledge of God in nature is insufficient for developing theology.

Fourth, perspectives of science and philosophy relate to how we interpret Genesis.

Fifth, there is a brief discussion of the mystery of God being hidden yet being known to human beings. God's self-revelation comes primarily through Scripture, but is also seen in Creation.

Finally, we should view the Bible as God-inspired, but also as a very human book. This dual nature of the Bible must be considered as we interpret Genesis. The main purpose of Genesis is to tell us about God. What it tells about nature is secondary, and is limited by the cultural, pre-scientific understanding of its human authors.

Placing current understanding of nature alongside the possible understandings of those who wrote the texts that have come to us is required for our faithful interpretation of Genesis.

It is still daylight at midnight. I am walking across the arctic tundra, in the direction of my elongated shadow. It is July 1993. The sun hangs low over the northern horizon and Arctic Ocean, but it will not set during my entire stay in Barrow, Alaska. At this most northern point of the United States, the sun shines continuously for almost three months in summer, but never rises for about two months in winter. What is a day, and what is a night in such a place?

Native Inuit children play outside at two o'clock in the morning. Some non-natives block their windows to achieve an artificial night. I watch a Snowy Owl land on a hump in the tundra, and wonder if a nest is nearby. A large shadow passes over me, and I look up to see a great dark bird. I almost stumble over a bed of bones that look like human skulls, femurs and hips. I wonder if these are really human or possibly seal bones. I remember stories, not often true, that the elderly who were becoming a burden wander away from the village in the dark of winter as a gesture of love to their survivors.

On the surface, Barrow depicts modern American culture, but the original Inuit culture pokes through the facade everywhere you look. Barrow's Mayor has a polar bear hide stretched on the side of his house and a partially butchered seal on an improvised table near his front door. I am a stranger in this place and to this culture.

The bone bed on the Alaskan tundra near Barrow, AK.

Perspective on What a Day Is

How I perceive the world is very different from the understanding of the elderly natives who have experienced a survival way of life, stretching back many generations. How do they experience time? Would evening and morning be one day? But what is an evening and morning when the sun never rises or sets for months? What would arguments about the length of days in Genesis 1 seem like to this culture?

My point is simple, but modern day readers of Genesis often ignore it. Understanding the culture of those who heard or read the original account of Genesis is critical to understanding its meaning. What assumptions and understandings are appropriate for interpreting Genesis? These culturally derived views must be considered in interpreting the text of Genesis, and to relate its text to theology and science.

How Did Genesis Communicate in the Beginning?

In the beginning, Genesis communicated clearly. For a thousand or more years, the early texts of Genesis made sense to readers of Abrahamic faiths—whether Jews, Christians, or Muslims. Many read and understood it quite literally. Few doubted that God created, or that Adam and Eve were the first parents of the human race. Most accepted the flood of Noah's day as the greatest natural disaster affecting life on earth. Other religions and cultures had different beginning stories, but these seemed alien to most persons in the western world. A broad spectrum of people, with many different cultures, from the Near East, to Europe, to North, and South America accepted the early Genesis text as the factual account of creation and human origin. How Genesis was interpreted theologically may have varied, but for the most part readers had similar views of the creation and flood as being acts of God.

Doubts raised about the reality of these ancient stories shook this simple foundation of faith like a series of earthquakes. Sometimes doubts arose when people became familiar with the myths of other peoples. Scholars shook the foundation by analyzing the historical development, grammatical and literary structure, and parallels of the original texts. Then along came scientists, who discovered a different story in the stars, the rocks of the earth, and evidences of past life. Archaeologists dug up the ruins of past civilizations and pieced together their stories. Soon, many educated people were no longer reading Genesis as a literal account of creation or the beginning of human life.

Millions still read early Genesis with unquestioning faith, but many others have felt a shattering blow to their childhood understanding of creation, Adam and Eve, and the worldwide flood. Others may have a distinct bias against a simple, literal understanding from the time they first became acquainted with these stories as part of western culture. Having learned of the Genesis story as part of their understanding of western culture may lead some to feel an intellectual superiority to the admittedly popular view of more fundamentalist Christians, who tend to take the Bible literally.

A few scholars in the conservative camp have defended the traditional understanding of Genesis. Some scientists of this persuasion have even tried to build a case for the "scientific creationism" popular in the United States among conservative Christians. They have attempted to rewrite modern science related to origins in a way that agrees with the earlier understanding of the creation and flood in Genesis. For the most part, these efforts have resulted in indifference, active scorn or alarm, from the majority of the scientific community.

The legal battles over public education teaching evolution have polarized faith and science in current American thought. As a result, some people insist on a literal view of the Genesis accounts as a proof of true faith.

This polarity results in an over-simplification of many different, faith-guided views of thoughtful Christians who find the biblical creation account and evolutionary theory to be irreconcilable. The truth is that many persons in the modern Western world, whether Christian or Jew, find significant value for faith in Genesis while accepting the major findings of scholars and scientists providing a different lens to view the texts.

Our reading of Genesis has been impacted by the development of science and by scholarly studies based on principles of scientific analysis.

Making sense of Genesis today requires some background as to the origin of Genesis. Who told or wrote these stories, and how does this relate to their being inspired by God? Who heard or read Genesis, and what cultural background affected them in how they understood its message? What does this mean for us who read Genesis in the beginning of the twenty-first century?

Who were the earliest people to whom the words of Genesis came? There is no simple answer to this question. A traditional answer has been that the Genesis account was revealed by God to Moses, who then wrote it for the Children of Israel. There are reasons to believe that Moses should be given some credit for the authorship of Genesis, including the creation and flood accounts, as well as the rest of the first five books known as the Pentateuch. This belief is traditional, and traditions had to begin somewhere. The beginning might well be in the simple fact that Moses wrote down such a text.

We know today that writing was already an old, well-developed human skill at the time of Moses, but reading was limited to a scholarly class who served the upper crust of society. A leader of stature, who had a good education of that time with any concern for propagating and perpetuating ideas, would probably choose to write as well as speak. This would have been especially true if the leader did not consider himself an eloquent speaker, as the Exodus record suggests was the case for Moses. The various texts of the Pentateuch either say that Moses wrote, or refer to Moses' writings. They do not precisely define the body of text that is his work, but clearly suggest that such works existed, and give reason to believe that they were valued enough to be preserved.

The purported character of Moses indicates that he would have been interested in the traditions of his people. Moses knew the traditions of his heritage, and compared them with those of other cultures. He may have been in a better position than we are to determine what was authentic, and what the true roots of his people were. After spending forty years in the mainstream of Egyptian culture and its religious mythological heritage, Moses must certainly have been curious, if not already knowledgeable, of his own heritage as he turned from Egyptian values to take on the identity of a people of his own flesh and blood.

Supposing Moses had ability in the scholarship of his day, he certainly had time and the setting in which to pursue what could enrich his chosen identity, after fleeing Egypt. He lived in the desert with a priest of a religion outside the Egyptian cultural stream. Priests were generally guardians, if not makers of cultural and religious knowledge. Moses' occupation as a shepherd gave him plenty of time for thought. He probably reevaluated all that he knew and had continued to learn. After forty years of such a life, what might have been his perspective been?

Moses' brother was another source of information about their religious and cultural heritage. When Moses returned to Egypt, his brother Aaron, said to have some stature as a speaker, came to meet him. This suggests some prior communication between them, likely not the first, if Moses was really interested in his religious identity. His brother seemed to have some standing among the elders of his people. Certainly Aaron could have been a good source to Moses in regard to his heritage.

An even more important event affected Moses' understanding and beliefs, and profoundly influenced what he would put in writing. At the burning bush, Moses met the God of his forebears, the God who gave Moses his ultimate identity and purpose. God communicated so that Moses got a clear message, one that was too plain for Moses. Moses was not ready to accept God's message. He only accepted it after God used considerable persuasion.

A scientific mind will ask how God communicated with Moses. There is no one scientific answer, but a God who could create the human voice could surely also produce God's own voice? The one who could give capacity for human thought could certainly also place God's own thoughts within human consciousness. In whatever way Moses perceived God's message, Moses knew it was God's message as certainly as one person knows the communication of another in relationship.

These arguments assume that biblical stories are to be taken at face value, that they depict experiences that happened even though they are expressed in ways that we do not fully comprehend, despite using critical thinking. Personal accounts about God go beyond the valid turf of science's ability to prove or refute. We may examine the subjective reporting of human experience and conclude that while Moses' experience may be unusual, it is certainly within the range of that reported by other human beings.

The Semitic culture of the Hebrews from the area of Mesopotamia has parallel creation accounts, many with a number of similarities as well as some major differences to these early Genesis accounts. Moses was likely in a position to write the Genesis accounts of creation, both from the standpoint of knowledge of such stories in his oral or written heritage and by communication from God. If the early written text of Genesis is dated from the time of Moses and not later, as many assert, earlier traditions related to the creation accounts suggest the possibility of prior sources. Moses' authorship does not preclude the use of other sources, and God's inspiration does not exclude such human effort.

The Oral and Written Form of Genesis Likely Changed

The Hebrew text did not remain frozen in its original form, without changes, from the time of Moses to modern day. Why should we not accept the textual and contextual evidence of further editing, perhaps even rewording, as language changed? These changes might well reflect the developing Hebrew language, culture and Jewish theology. The human element behind our present Hebrew text of Genesis should not detract from a divine presence inspiring and preserving God's communication in living relation to believers of many generations from Moses to us.

Some similarities of this reworking of a text in a changing language can be found in the story of the past 500 years of the development of the English Bible. If the human creature can communicate across millennia to other humans, how much more can the Creator of humans and communication also express a message across time to us!

We can be open to literary and historical critical methodologies as long as the internal text is not made to stand on its head in an inversion of its truth. In our search for how these Genesis accounts came to be, Moses may well be somewhere in the middle of the trail, even if he is one of its brighter markers.

The track of our story cannot be fully documented by biblical chronology alone. Archaeological, geological and even astronomical dating methods must be used if we intend to go back to the opening statement of Genesis, "In the beginning. . ." Moses' lifetime took place somewhere around 1200 to 1400 B.C.E. Going back an additional four to six hundred years takes us to the Hebrew patriarchs, Jacob, Isaac, and finally Abraham.[1] From Abraham to Moses is a history, if it were told, as long as that of the so-called "discovery" by Columbus of America to the current American experience.

Genesis: A Family Tradition?

Perhaps the beginning of the Genesis account is a tradition related to a particular family. This family may have traced its genealogy to Adam as listed in later genealogies in Genesis. What is so significant about this family tradition is that it is not only a revelation from God, but it is a revelation of God. In Genesis 14, Abram and Melchizedek identify God as the Creator and Possessor of heaven and earth. Such identification of God grew out of their traditions.

Perhaps Adam was the one who first received this revelation, and first experienced what it was to know God personally. This would indeed put Adam in a unique position with respect to all human beings. He had an encounter of the first kind, a God-encounter. The garden story indicates that God went to considerable lengths to prepare a setting for this first encounter with the human beings he created. It appears to be an encounter, at first, with a man, but later includes a woman. At some point in the story the humans are named, Adam and Eve.

Did the early accounts that are now found in Genesis pass down from generation to generation through all those years to Moses? Possibly. The mechanism of transmission would likely have been oral tradition, but some written accounts may also have existed. Oral tradition often has remarkable reliability, but may also allow for creative interpretation. Moses may have given the accounts an extended written form for the children of Israel and the mixed multitudes that accompanied them in their exodus from Egypt. Certainly this diverse group of people needed some basic understanding of God for their journey in addition to what would become their own experience of God as Yahweh. The experience of the Exodus had already-existing roots that would form this group's budding national identity.

The first account of Genesis Chapter One might have come out of conversations between God and Adam and possibly Eve. Although God was the supremely great communicator, God had a problem. Adam's pre-scientific vocabulary would only permit a limited account of the wonders of the creation process. God could and did communicate that God was sole Creator, and that creation itself should not be confused with God. Creation had a beginning. Adam could have shared this knowledge of God with others, and from this and other God encounters, we have the rest of the book of Genesis.

There is no proof that this is the way it happened, or that these revelations did not come until long after Moses, but why not begin at the beginning, "a very good place to begin?" Likely these first accounts were oral traditions, lodged deeply in the Hebrew memory long before they were written down or became the form we have today.

Scholars often view these stories as myths in the sense of symbolic language communicating transcendent meaning within a culture, revealing its cosmic dimensions.[2] The term "myth" may make some of us feel uncomfortable because we think of myths as "lying fables"—as the meaning of myths appears in some epistles of Paul and Peter. However, there is certainly truth in the taking of these accounts as transcendent stories, revealing cosmic dimensions.

The first two accounts of "creation" are part of the primordial history of the earliest generations of the world and humankind. Chapters 1-11 set the stage for the call of Abraham. "The creation story serves as a preface not just to Genesis but to the entire Hebrew Bible."[3]

Commentators on the Pentateuch are pessimistic about finding scientific and external historical data to support the historicity of its text. Terence E. Fretheim, author of *The Pentateuch, Interpreting Biblical Texts* is one author I refer to frequently. He is a widely respected Old Testament scholar. (See his helpful comment below).

Details in the Pentateuchal texts have not been corroborated and many difficulties remain. However, archaeological findings do not prove (or disprove) the truth of the Bible. Certainly, some genuine memories of Israel's early history have been preserved.[4]

Israelite ancestors are often described in unattractive terms. Genesis reflects the meaning(s) of the Israelite story, and it is historical in that sense. Though this reflection may often stem from times *subsequent* to the entry into Canaan, it has continuities with earlier times. The authors and editors no doubt used their imaginations freely. But, even where the judgment of the historiographers may be negative, the material retains its import as a word of and about God.[5]

Another commentator asks the question of how important it is for faith that stories reported in the text actually happened. Truth may be conveyed by fiction as well as fact. Jesus' parables were powerful truth-telling stories whether they were actual historical experience or not. Fretheim notes a degree of objectivity in simply telling the story.

It is an act of the imagination to think that authors and editors imagined private conversations. In verbal cultures, the telling of exact words is part of telling the whole story. Our modern-day culture is more likely to forget the exact words and supply them by imagination.

There is a lack of agreement on the importance of historicity for the significance of the bible texts. Just as some Bible readers favor the traditional KJV, others prefer the more literal rendering of the NRSV, some the more thought-to-thought translation of the NIV, and still others the contemporary imaginative presentation of *The Message*.

What Is The Significance Of History-Like Variations?

There are several additional observations to be considered. While the stories of Genesis 1-11 may be understood critically as myths because they represent aspects of the world that are timeless (such as the pain of work and childbirth, hostilities between gardeners and shepherds, the rise of cities, and development of multiplicity of languages), they also reflect a larger historical and cultural tradition. This tradition has various parallels in Near Eastern Literature, although the biblical stories are radically different in several significant ways.[6] Scholars may not have pinned down the relationships as to succession of these various documents, but there is the question of an original common tradition, and whether such tradition sprang from the imagination or experience of a people with a common cultural and biological source.

The biblical text places these stories in a history-like context of people with a common genealogical lineage. Thomas W. Mann, Hebrew Bible professor and well-known pastor and author, in *The Book of the Torah* notes this larger context:

"The linking of originally independent stories into a progressive series means a fundamental change has taken place. Each story is not simply an incident that 'occurred' in primordial timelessness, and the meaning of each story is no longer limited to a description of 'the way we are.'" The meaning of the individual stories is now significantly augmented in that they have become prologue to the rest of the Pentateuch. Although we cannot say that these myths have been converted into history, we can say that they have been transformed into a kind of "history-like" narrative."[7]

Another perspective might be to suggest that the linkage is not artificial but simply an accretion of experiences of a people with common roots and culture. Of course the stories from that experience have been chosen because of their overall significance to the biblical text as we now have it.

These parallel stories need to be viewed from a perspective of their role in Israelite history. They must also be seen in the larger context of time and place. We cannot ignore scholarship of the past several hundred years that has suggested alternate answers to the questions about how the Pentateuch was formed. Joseph Blenkinsopp, whose research focuses on the Pentateuch, draws this conclusion in trying to salvage past scholarly work:

". . . it is true that the documentary hypothesis has increasingly shown to be flawed, and will survive, if at all, only in greatly modified form, but that does not mean that we should ignore the results of the last two centuries of investigation. Our task is to find better ways of understanding how the Pentateuch came to be without writing off the real advances of our predecessors."[8]

There is the possibility of an over-all editing or redaction of the original accounts into our present Pentateuch. However, this does not greatly affect how we understand and interpret Genesis 1-3. There are scholarly arguments about possible prior oral sources, and how they might be dated, but there is no clear consensus that would be considered authoritative. Readers of the Pentateuch need not become informed historical critics in order to have confidence in an interpretation of the first chapters of Genesis or the Pentateuch as a whole. The following analysis by Fretheim is helpful:

"Critics are probably more confident in their historical statements than they ought to be. Historical data is quite sparse and difficult to interpret. Studies of Israel, its history and its literature become dated quickly."[9]

The most lasting results appear to be some agreement about priestly material in the Pentateuch and similar material.[10] Critical analysis suggests two primary genres in the Pentateuch—narrative and law. Narrative predominates in Genesis through Exodus 19.[11]

Other approaches led to further development of a history of traditions approach. Fretheim continues on to say that there is a recognition that the Pentateuch was shaped by theological, religious and institutional concerns. The speeches in Deuteronomy are examples of this. Here, persons of faith were speaking a word of and about God to other people of faith.[12]

Fretheim suggests that there is little scholarly consensus as to the historical reliability of these texts. "Such conclusions have made some readers nervous, for the authority of the Bible seems thereby to be called into question. Yet, the truth value of biblical texts is not necessarily related to their historicity (witness parables, for example)."[13]

The stories of Genesis 1-3 are not history in the sense of criteria used by modern historians, nor should we think that this is the intent of the texts.

Language of error/inaccuracy ought not be used to devalue the Genesis texts, just as one would not misprize the imaginative retelling of biblical stories for children. Israelites likely thought that these traditions were inherited from ancient times, but no evidence exists that they evaluated them in terms of historicity. The narrators certainly transmitted matters that did not correspond to the facts, but this reality should be evaluated in terms of purposes that were not historiographical.[14]

Scholars do recognize that Israel viewed these first stories in a larger context of their history, and they were likely the first peoples to do so. "It seems reasonable to conclude that in the first nine books of the Hebrew Bible, Israel anticipated the Greeks in producing a national history traced back to creation and the mythic origins of humanity."[15] This again raises the issue whether this perception of creation and human origin was fiction or the result of the accumulation of human experience from an original event and revelation of God to human beings. The truth of the stories bears the marks of actual events and not simply the mythic truth of fiction.

Parallel Development of Historical Texts

A similar case to the development of the early Genesis accounts is the development of the account of *The Trojan War, A New History* by Barry Strauss. Most written testimonies about the Trojan War date to the start of the Archaic Age at the end of the Roman Empire. We must look backward to understand. The times before the start of the Archaic Age are known collectively as the Greek Dark Ages (ca. 1150-750 B.C.). "Dark" in this context means no written history, but evidence uncovered by archaeologists, which sheds light on the era.[16]

Strauss, a student of the classics, probes this evidence to give a modern account of what likely happened at Troy some 3,000 years ago. He pieces together the archeological and classical evidence in a way that gives one a sense of what this war may have been like in actual human experience. The original source has to be these actual human experiences, although they were written down at a later time.

The most important texts about the Trojan War are two long poems, called epics because they tell of the heroic deeds of men long ago. The *Iliad* is set near the end of the Trojan War, and it covers about two months of the conflict. The *Odyssey* relates the hero Odysseus's long, hard trip home from Troy; it adds only a few additional details about the Trojan War. Both of these texts are attributed to a Greek poet named Homer.

Other poems about early Greece were written in Archaic Greece. Known as the "Epic Cycle," six of these poems narrate the parts of the Trojan War missing from the *Iliad* and the *Odyssey* . . . . Unfortunately, only a few quotations from the Epic Cycle, as well as brief summaries survive today. Many later writers in ancient times used these and other sources to comment on Homer.[17]

Historical evidence of Genesis

The evidence for the Biblical text we know as Genesis is better documented than that of Homer or the Epic Cycle. Biblical archeology is extensive, but it cannot take us back to the Garden of Eden as well as the archeology of Troy takes us back to the Trojan War. In neither case do we have known artifacts from the persons involved, but we may have some evidence from the culture of their times. In both cases, actual experiences were first told as stories, and became oral traditions before they were preserved in written form. Strauss concludes as follows:

"In his exaggerations and his honesty, Homer is truer to the age of the Trojan War than is usually recognized. Such texts preserve the truth: a way of war that was sometimes low-intensity, often devious, and always squalid. Using oral tradition and also perhaps non-Greek written sources, Homer preserves these truths, even though Troy fell centuries before his lifetime.[18]

Genesis: Stories of Human Experiences With God

My own hypothesis is that the original stories in the Genesis texts grew out of actual human experiences with God, and were not simply myths written by some later visionary. Like Homer's account of the Trojan War and Barry Strauss' recent history of that war, Genesis preserves for us stories from the lives and oral accounts of the experience of early ancestors.

The Genesis story is much older than the Trojan War. Extensive supporting evidence is lacking, but it appears to hark back to early ancestors of the Hebrew people. This certainly cannot be proven in a historical or scientific sense. However, there may be little difference of how the heavens and earth were viewed by those who first gave an oral account from the views of the priestly scholars, who prepared written copies of the Genesis texts.

Until the blossoming of science over the past 500 years, many Genesis readers had not been greatly affected by the more scientifically enlightened view of planet earth and the astronomical universe.

Much of what most people think of Genesis is from impressions and traditions that are not actually supported by the Genesis account.

The same is true of Homer's account of the Trojan War. "But if the resulting picture builds on Homer, it differs quite a bit from the impression most readers get from his poems. And "impression" is the right word, because much conventional wisdom about the war, from Achilles' heel to Cassandra's warnings, is not in Homer at all."[19]

Which Biases do we bring to Genesis?

A careful look at Genesis should be through eyes that are not tinted by past impressions and traditions not actually supported by the accounts of Genesis. We need to think carefully about the perspectives we bring when we read the stories of Genesis. Donald Jacobs, a missionary anthropologist who gave his whole life to the emerging church around the world, has words of wisdom for us:

"I illustrate this by what happened to me on one of my many trips to Somalia. I was walking alone on a high bluff near the sea, looking east. Few morning skies are as crystal-clear as daybreak skies in Somalia. I could see for miles out to sea. As I stood there, I saw something that astounded me. As the first sliver of sun appeared I had the distinct sensation that the sea before me was going down and down, allowing more of the sun to appear. I was riding the earth downward! When I got my bearings I heard myself saying, "The sun does not come up. The earth goes down!" It is true; the sun was there all the time!

I was nurtured all the time on the fantasy that the sun comes up. It is even enshrined in the English language. What do I do now? The earth goes down; it just looks like the sun is coming up. Now and again, as I tried to see things from new perspectives, I recalled that morning in Somalia. It is there in my mind as a metaphor. Question your presuppositions. Some are right; some are not. Bring them out and look at them honestly."[20]

Chapter 2

In the Beginning God Created

Which translation do we use?

"In the Beginning God Created Heaven and Earth." (KJB)
These words from the King James Version of the Bible, (KJB), begun in 1604 and completed in 1611, are in mostly out-of-date English four hundred years later, but sounded great in the world of Shakespeare.

The Standard Jewish Bible, (SJB), Tanakh 1985, prepared by keepers of the Ancient Hebrew as well as Modern Hebrew and English, the Jewish Publication Society, render the same Hebrew words as:

"When God began to create heaven and earth-" (SJB)

A widely accepted translation by reputable scholars of the National Council of the Churches of Christ, the New Revised Standard Version, (NRSV), dated 1989, renders it:

"In the beginning when God created the heavens and the earth," (NRSV)

The New International Version, (NIV), 1978, translated by over a hundred scholars, including two of my own professors from the New York International Bible Society translates the same Hebrew as:

"In the beginning God created the heavens and the earth." (NIV)

It may seem picayune to most readers, but we could ask, "Is there one heaven or are there multiple heavens? Also is creation past tense "created," or is God still creating? Is the verse interpreted as "when God began to create" only referring to the first events of creation, ones that will be followed by other creation events?

God the Creator of Functions, Not Things

Most of us have always thought of God creating material things. John Walton, an Old Testament scholar and student of the ancient world in the book *"The Lost World of Genesis One"* suggests that God was creating functions. We modern materialists, with a worldview created by material science, can hardly conceive of the thought pattern of the ancient world of Genesis, which was primarily concerned with creating functions, not things. Let me illustrate this for you by way of a familiar Bible story from Genesis Chapter 41:

One of the mightiest men in the ancient world, the Pharaoh of Egypt, is greatly troubled by a dream about good and bad heads of wheat and good and bad cattle. None of Pharaoh's retinue of wise men is able to interpret Pharaoh's dream. One of the wise men remembers Joseph, a Hebrew slave who had been in prison with the wise man. Joseph had explained the wise man's own dream, and Joseph's interpretation was shown to be true by the wise man's restoration to Pharaoh's court.

Joseph is summoned to court immediately and told Pharaoh's dream. Joseph explains to Pharaoh that God revealed to Pharaoh that there would be seven bountiful years followed by seven famine years. Joseph's interpretation was so convincing and significant that Pharaoh immediately believed it. Pharaoh and his counselors must have known that they were facing a national crisis.

This was Joseph's opportunity, and God had prepared him for it. He could not stop the famine, but he could expound the functions needed to avert national disaster. Appoint a head man, discreet and wise, who will appoint officers over all Egypt to take a fifth of the crops of the good harvests and preserve them in city stores to sell during the famine years.

Pharaoh is so impressed by Joseph that he appoints him power over all Egypt, next in power to the Pharaoh himself, with authority to put the functions Joseph proposed into effect.

For the sake of status, Joseph was married into a leading Egyptian family. Joseph may not have even picked up a single grain of wheat to put it in storage, but what all Egypt knew and cared about was that Joseph had established and put into operation a lifesaving function to save them from starvation. Of course, it took wheat or other grain to do this. But Joseph was not making the grain.

Eventually the function Joseph instituted saved the lives of Joseph's father and that of his brothers, whose envy and vengeance had made it possible for Joseph to rise to a position for which they would bow before him.

John Walton assures us that creation in Genesis is about functions primarily, not about the objects or plants or animals, or humans that make up our world. In the first three days God creates functions, and in the second set of three days God appoints the functionaries to carry out what God intended. We should no longer think of creating functionaries as making the material objects, but as giving those functions in the same way Pharaoh did not create Joseph, but created Joseph's authority to function as Pharaoh's viceroy or deputy ruler.

This was the worldview of the ancient Hebrews and their contemporaries and of most people until the revolutions of developing science led to our own materialistic worldview. In short, we will not understand the Genesis account of creation unless we can return to the worldview of Pharaoh, Joseph and their contemporaries.

Modern science and the stories of Genesis can live with each other if we recognize what each has to contribute to our understanding and what the limitations of each might be. The challenge is to tell both stories in language that is as simple as possible for all to understand.

Regardless of how the beginning words of Genesis are translated into English, Biblical scholars do agree that the Hebrew Bible, unlike the creation myths of other contemporary cultures, tell of only one Creator, God. This one God is responsible for creating every function and every material thing that exists or has ever existed. This one God already exists at the beginning of all creation. In other words, this is a theological story about God just as the story about Pharaoh's dream is really about Pharaoh and his authority to make Joseph second to Pharaoh in royal power. This, of course, eventually became the fulfillment of Joseph's own dreams that his brothers' sheaves of grain would bow down to Joseph's sheaf and that the sun, moon and eleven stars would bow down to him.

Genesis ultimately tells us that we should worship God and worship God alone. This is the biblical story we wish to tell. We also want to tell the story of science—a story that is not derived from the Bible, but which can enrich our understanding of God, as well as our knowledge that material existence depends upon God.

Today's science has a lot to say about the topic of creation. It believes that there was a material beginning of the heaven and earth, meaning our universe.

Scientists mostly speculate about the existence or non-existence of God because science does not hear God thundering His words of revelation. They do often speak about God, because God-qualities have a lot to do with human values. We human beings are not just remarkable computing machines that engage in strictly scientific reasoning, but we constantly make value judgments, judgments that affect our wellbeing. We create legal systems to help maintain our social order and wellbeing as a human society and for the welfare of other living things.

We have at least two rails for the track that carries the train of our theological and legal thought. One rail supports wheels related to the meaning and purpose of life for the desired outcomes to lift our spirits. The other rail supports humans' means to alter and control the objects in our lives for desired physical outcomes. The train itself is driven by abstract reasoning and symbolic manipulation, both in us and in communication with other beings. Science, philosophy and theology wonder how we got to be as we are and what will become of us. These musings drive the train that gives us our human perspective on our world and our lives.

History of the Science of Creation

There is a long story as to how science came to talk about the beginning of the universe. For those not ready for detailed scientific analysis, I will give only a brief sketch of that history. One significant step in this scientific journey was to realize that the earth was not flat, but roughly a sphere with a measurable diameter in English measurement of about 8,000 miles. This concept of earth as a sphere was heresy to many Bible readers because the worldview of the cultures of biblical authors was that of a flat earth.

Steps that followed were the realization that earth was really a planet of relatively small size, in a solar system where the earth is in motion on its axis, and in revolution around the sun which is like other stars, but much closer to us than stars. This realization was considered a double and even triple heresy since the biblical earth seemed to be motionless, and at a central position in God's creation. Bible believers would quote Joshua as saying "Sun, stand still!" By now, most believers have come to some understanding that the Bible language speaks as to how things appear, and even that the biblical style of writing was the necessary way to communicate to people of the times in which the Bible was written.

Since the advent of large telescopes, science has shown that we are part of a spiral-shaped galaxy of stars we see in our night sky as the Milky Way. Our solar system appears to have no place or form of special significance in its own galaxy, and certainly has no great importance among the billions of galaxies that we now know make up the universe. This knowledge of the larger universe seems to estrange us further from the Bible, but also deals a telling blow to our egocentric view of human importance in creation.

Recently, scientists have come to understand that the universe itself is expanding like a balloon that is being blown up. Science has even measured the time from which the universe seems to have started from nothing in what has popularly become known as 'the big bang.' Science itself or at least some scientists found the thought of a big bang disturbing, because it seemed too much like an act of creation. They proposed alternative theories of multiple chance universes, or that of a steady state universe, all of which have landed on the dust heap of untenable scientific speculation.

The ongoing march of scientific knowledge has even measured background radiation left over from the explosive beginning of the universe. It has determined that the beginning of the universe was almost 14 billion year ago. Bible believers, who took the Biblical genealogical years literally in thinking that creation was about 6,000 years ago, were dealt another blow. Geological science shocked these believers into strongly protesting scientific evidence of around four and a half billion years of earth's age.

Many kinds of new data and speculations continue to arise about this old universe in which we live. There are serious conversations about black holes, dark matter and dark energy. Some scientists even think that there might be billions of other universes that we can never know about. Because the properties at the beginning of our universe are so finely tuned to produce the particular conditions needed for life, again seem to indicate that a creator had a hidden hand in its beginning. A chance beginning of the known universe would require billions or more big bangs for a roulette of new universes to produce one with such livable conditions, opening new questions for both science and theology.

Knowing God the Creator

"From the time the world was created, people have seen the earth and sky and all that God made. They can clearly see his invisible qualities—his eternal power and divine nature. So they have no excuse whatsoever for not knowing God." Romans 1:20 (NLT)

Human beings are creative, and we recognize this characteristic trait in other species. Other creatures manipulate their environment in ways that could be said to be creative. A good education and even our media challenge us to create. We associate creativity with intelligence, and even rate ourselves at the top of the animal kingdom in a large part on the basis of human creativity. Is it any wonder that at least some, if not most, of our early ancestors came to postulate a creator for the world, with all its variety? Three of the world's great religions, Judaism, Christianity and Islam, have developed theologies about God as Creator. Other religions and some major thinkers of the enlightenment and modern science have observed the processes of the natural world and concluded that they had no ultimate rational meaning, therefore, there was no need for a creator.

Is there a Creator or no Creator?

Our discussion asks the question: "Is there, or is there not a Creator?" Are Jews, Christians and Muslims, who all affirm the Genesis text given above, correct? Is Paul, the great Jewish Christian theologian, who would also be affirmed by Muslims, incorrect in his assertion about God in the text of Romans? What do you think and why do you believe what you think?

When I look at a complicated modern device, I believe that it had an inventor. But I also recognize that there is a history of the processes used to develop the device in its current form. I may have no clue who it was who invented a wheeled vehicle, but I believe that if its inventor could see a modern automobile, he or she would recognize some relation to the original cart. Henry Ford would know that a modern car is related to his Model T. If Ford were to watch the processes for assembling a car today, he would see a relationship to his own original assembly line. Yet the cart inventor and Henry Ford would both be mystified by much of the mechanisms and functions related to our current automobile industry.

I have created a few things myself. Right now I am working on building a grandmother clock. Of course I am not its original inventor, but what I am making will be uniquely mine. Although some clockmakers would view my clock (if I succeed in making it) as amateurish and primitive, I think that I would be accepted as the maker of this particular clock.

So it is reasonable that when I look at what Genesis 1:1 calls "the heavens and the earth" that I accept the assertion that God created them in the beginning. But you might say that God was not necessary; heaven and earth came about by natural processes. I would agree with you, but I would also ask whether there is some degree of logic and reason in natural processes. I expect that you would agree that there is. If you were a scientist, you might have all kinds of well-reasoned explanations revolving around the origin of the heavens and the earth. You might even have complex mathematical equations from physics to explain the origin of matter, stars, planets and the universe, or even the possibility of multiple universes, dark matter, and dark energy.

I think humans are highly intelligent. I would think that God is even more highly intelligent, and that complex processes are part of the natural order. From the knowledge of the development of science, we know that we don't have all the answers. If we could come back in a thousand years and investigate science, we might be as amazed as the early cart-maker would be seeing a modern car. I am amazed at human creativity, but even more amazed at God's creativity. In conclusion, both the object and the process that created it, require a Creator.

Instinct and Ingenuity – Planning or Chance?

If I see a bird's nest, I affirm that a bird made it, even though I might grant that instinct, not human-like reasoning, was involved in making the nest. If I see a great building or a large jetliner, I affirm that they were made by human ingenuity. What is different about instinct and ingenuity? Instinct is hardwired or programmed into the animal's brain.

How does instinct get programmed? Programmed by the chance of evolutionary success? How did ingenuity get into the human brain? Is it not a kind of ability to program new programs so that humans can make many kinds of buildings and jetliners? We see that ingenuity came about by the chance of evolutionary success.

I would assert that God causes a bird's instinct and a human's ingenuity. Whether we have hardwired programming or the ability to program new programs, I believe that this is not only by chance, but that the programming also requires a programmer, who I believe, is God, the creator. We either assert that nature comes about ultimately by chance or by planning. I affirm God's planning, though that does not rule out some degree of what we might call chance.

Chance and Determination

I look at it like this: I have played golf only a few times, and I am not very skilled at getting the ball in the hole. It doesn't take a professional player to beat me at golf. I don't have good control of the muscles required to take an expert swing with the golf club to hit the ball, so there appears to be a lot of chance in where the ball goes. In addition, I am not a good judge of how a breeze might affect the flight of the ball, or of how the surface of the course and its slope might affect how the ball will roll. Pro players have much better control because they have more experience and knowledge about these things. Even so, the best player's odds of making a hole in one every time is not great. There is still significant chance in the sport. However, I do know that how the ball travels is controlled by the laws of motion and physics related to traveling in the air or rolling on a surface, and also related to the power of my muscles and their control.

Even the best player does not completely understand or control all of the factors that determine a ball's movement. Every shot appears to involve chance, but a physicist would affirm that the laws of motion ultimately determine how and where the ball goes. Come to think of it, there wouldn't be much attraction to a sport that did not involve both elements of chance and elements of determination.

I observe both elements of chance and elements of determination in creation or nature, however you define it. I also believe that God planned nature this way. There are many theological arguments related to determination or free will for human beings that I will not pursue here. I do think that chance opens up the possibility of free will, but in the end, I believe that God is the supreme player regarding life, and that someday God's will "will be done on earth as it is in heaven."

Reasons Why Some Reject God the Creator

A large theological question is that of human accountability or responsibility. One reason for denying God may be our desire to be free of all accountability and responsibility. In the Romans text,

Paul affirms that we have no excuse for not knowing God. In other passages of scripture, he ties unbelief to moral decay.

Hitler's German debacle resulted from an ill-advised and inappropriate application of evolution to morality, thinking that his desired goal of an Aryan master race justified any means. His desired end and his means are both called into question by a larger humanity, as well as religiously based ethics. I can accept that an evolutionist can devise societal based ethics. However, I cannot imagine that societal ethics, with all the foibles of humankind, would be better than God-based ethics. The Bible, as a whole, may well come from God's work to draw humankind into higher ethics and into a personal relationship with God.

Humans' Relationship with God

This may be the most significant issue related to creation: "What is the Creator's relationship to creation and especially to human beings, including you and me?" Most human beings place themselves at the top of other creatures and life on this planet. Do we matter to God? Does God communicate with us? Does God love or hate us? Do we love or hate God? Does God have attributes that we commonly attribute primarily to human beings?

From personal experience and observation of others, I know that what we "create" is important to us. The creative process involves both qualities of mind, emotion and what we may call spirit. The Romans text affirms that we can know about God's eternal power and divine nature by observing nature. This is similar to learning about another person by learning to know their creations.

I find both the Genesis and the Romans texts to be true. I have given only a few examples of why I believe this. Many others have written on this topic, as well. There are libraries of books, both ancient and recent, that address this topic from many angles. My goal is to stimulate thought, the desire to search more deeply, and to honestly consider the reasons for beliefs or unbeliefs. This is not a topic to be taken lightly. It is a matter of how we live and die.

Do Explanations Refute God Acting in Creation?

I have been using the term 'create' in the broad general sense. Theologically, some may use 'create' in a more restricted sense. First applying it to God alone, and second applying it only to the first of a kind made by God. By that logic, persons would answer the old mind teaser about the chicken and the egg by saying that the bird came before the egg, because God 'created' the bird to lay the egg, and thus produced all the subsequent generations of birds, which are hatched, not 'created'! This argument would go on to say that only Adam and Eve were 'created' and all the rest of us were conceived and born. This viewpoint neatly demarcates a line between so-called 'creation' as a one-time act of God, and the natural processes that are involved in all subsequent generations of life we observe today.

The opening words of Genesis 1:1 are: "In the beginning God 'created' the heaven and the earth." Many believers think that God was before the universe, and that God was the Creator of every thing that has ever existed. To others, these words of Genesis are but the rusty squeaking of tired old wheels on biblical tracks being torn apart by the advance of science. Both viewpoints assume that the words are understood in today's world, by today's people, but this may not be true in either case. These words originally written in ancient Hebrew, which almost none of us can read today, do not even have the same translation into English by scholars who can read them.

God Known in Relationship

The Bible does not start with an argument for God, as if it needed some philosophical defense of God's existence: it begins with the presumption that God is. The initial speaker or writer of these words appears to know God in a relational way. How foolish it would be to try to prove the existence of a person that we know relationally! The Bible is not a tract trying to convince an atheist that there is a God. In the beginning, we have the word of a theist, probably spoken or written to an audience of theists. "Also, the writer presupposes the existence and basic character of God."[21]

The message of the Bible is a far-reaching one about the character of God. God is Creator. The scope of God's creative work is all that the human audience can know or imagine: heaven and earth. For many, many years of human existence the earth, *"erets"* in Hebrew, was the extent of land and seas, without known end. The heavens were all that was perceived to be above the earth; sky, clouds and sun by day, and the mysterious moon and bodies or points of light by night, which seemed to transverse the sky in the same way the sun did by day. The stupendous point being made by the bible text is that God created all of that! Fretheim states:

"'Heaven and earth' specifies the ordered universe [see Ps 89:11], the totality of the world in which everything has its proper place and function. This phrase also testifies to a bipartite structure, wherein 'the heavens are the LORD's heavens, but the earth he has given to human beings' [Ps 115:16]. The heavens are an integral aspect of the world *as created*. Other texts show that heaven as God's abode is built into the very structure of the created order. . . ."[22]

The beginning presumption of God as creator is echoed later in Exodus in God's words to Moses at the burning bush, "I AM WHO I AM." (Ex. 3:14a) The words of Exodus, chapter three, also assume that Moses knows something about the relationship of his ancestors with God, the history of which is found in the stories of Genesis.

Only God could be present to know the "beginning." In its very beginning, Biblical theology is a revelation of God that appears to come from God. The second theological statement is that God is the Creator of all things. Biblical theology shows that it is in God's very character to be the Creator. This idea is reiterated in many passages of the Hebrew Bible, particularly in the Psalms. In the Gospel of John, it is stated in a deliberate way, parallel to the opening words of Genesis, "In the beginning was the Word, and the Word was with God, and the Word was God. He was in the beginning with God. All things came into being through him, and without him not one thing came into being." (John 1:1-3a) Another astounding claim is being made. All that exists, apart from God who created it, had a beginning.

Cosmology is a science that presumes to say something about the beginning of the universe, which is our modern term for heaven and earth. The simplest assumption of cosmology is that the matter and energy that compose the universe are eternal. One of the early significant discoveries of science was that matter is conserved, not created or destroyed, in chemical reactions. This discovery was superseded by the famous equation concluded by Einstein, $E = MC^2$, which shows that matter and energy are interchangeable, and that it is their sum total that is conserved. So how could there be a beginning of matter and energy? [23]

Astronomical data that showed stars and galaxies drifting apart on a universal scale led to the concept of the expanding universe. The converse of expansion, when looking backward in time, is contraction. The surprising conclusion was that the universe appeared to start from a point somewhere in the distant past. It had a beginning. This was not easily accepted in scientific circles. However, evidence of a beginning became so overwhelming, that a "Big Bang" cosmology was born.

The Big "Bloom"

The term "big bang" is something of a misnomer. A member of a Senior Men's Sunday school class I was teaching once noted that explosions break things to pieces, rather than form new things. The "big bloom" might be a more apt term, painting a picture of the development of an intricately detailed flower from an almost invisible initial bud. A bloom requires the feeding of new material into the bud in order to grow the flower.

The big bang contained the substance and energy of what is now the universe in compact form. From this it expanded into the present structure of the universe and its contents of stars, galaxies, clusters of galaxies, and so forth. In its complete form, the theory is a complex of mathematical models that explain this unfolding of the universe, from the development of its shape and content from subatomic particles to atoms of the elements and molecules, to stars and planets, to galaxies and galactic clusters, and to many wildly wonderful things like quasars and black holes that peak our imaginations with their mysteries. The mathematical model also proposes possible measurements that yield an estimate of the age of our universe, which is now considered to be 13.7 billion years old. Of course, science is still undergoing new developments, which is a healthy condition.

All of this should not be taken to mean that Genesis anticipates the particular theory in the forms known to current science. What Genesis states and what science can or has discovered, is that the universe had a beginning. The universe as we know it is not eternal. This basic idea of a beginning of the world was communicated, by God, to the person who reported the text of Genesis.

There are many scholarly arguments related to the exact interpretation and grammar of the first two verses of Genesis. Scholars and translators have taken three or more positions regarding the grammatical relationship of the first two verses. They boil down to whether God in the beginning created the heaven and earth out of nothing[24], or whether the beginning refers to God bringing order out of something that God had already created.[25] In any case, the text states that heaven and earth had a beginning, which does relate to the scientific concept of the beginning of the universe.

God's Reworking Dark Formless Materials into Earth

Genesis 1:2a reads:

> "And the earth was without form and void; and darkness was upon the face of the deep." (KJV)

> "-the earth being unformed and void, with darkness over the surface of the deep . . ." (SJB)

> "The earth was a formless void and darkness covered the face of the deep . . ." (NRSV)

> "Now the earth was formless and empty, darkness was over the surface of the deep . . ." (NIV)

What is clear in this verse is a change of perspective from God at the beginning, to God ready to work on the earth. Genesis' account is not of planet Earth as it exists today, nor of a flat and fixed planet at the center of the ancient world and heavens. Genesis talks about an earth that was dark, without the time-related element of alternating light and dark that permits the concept of days. The ancients would have understood that the earth was not organized and functionally orderly. Picture God looking at the earth as my six-year-old grandson who looked at my desk and exclaimed, "This desk is a mess! It needs to be cleaned up!"

At times, my desk does look a little more "cleaned up." What would it be like for the earth to be "cleaned up"? The Bible and science have at least this in common: our human wonderings run on tracks related to our thoughts and feelings. We agree that the earth should support life, particularly human life. This is the earth that both the Bible and Science know and love an earth with living things! So what is the God of the Bible going to do about the "messy earth", and is this God aware of what is needed to bring order and life?

The next words of Genesis in 1:2b say:

> "And the Spirit of God moved upon the face of the waters." (KJV)

> "and a wind from God sweeping over the water_" (SJB)

> "while a wind from God swept over the face of the waters." (NRSV)

> "and the Spirit of God was hovering over the waters." (NIV)

It is clear that God has shown up. We can suppose that God is assessing the 'mess' that is found in a dark formless void on the surface of God's beginning earth. Theologically, the various translations raise an issue about the nature of God's presence. KJV and NIV say that the Spirit of God is present, but the SJB and the NRSV mention only a wind from God. In the Hebrew language the word here associated with God can mean both wind and/or spirit, so we are left with the mystery that both translations may be correct. Christians, but not Jews, talk about several persons in the one being of God, including the Holy Spirit and Christ, or God the Father, Son and Holy Spirit, which is admittedly a paradoxical concept.

At least God is or has been active in relation to the 'earth mess'. Was it literally water, good old chemical H_2O, as we moderns think of it, or at least wet water as the early readers would know it, or is water simply used to describe the condition of an unstable mess? I tend to think the latter, but the wet stuff might also do the trick.

The second verse of Genesis appears to shift perspective from a framework of the universe, to that of earth in particular, in an attempt to describe the early earth and how God related to it. What is clear is that the beginning earth was not at all like the familiar world that we humans know and love. This makes sense from a non-scientific perspective, and from a scientific one. It does leave us to wonder how the earth became what we know it to be today.

Science does tell us quite a bit about the formation of the earth. In the Big Bang, the matter or even energy that would become the earth cannot be identified with our familiar rocks, minerals and seas. In the early stage of matter, there were primarily subatomic components of hydrogen and helium atoms. These formed the early stars. The more complex atoms of the earth, such as iron, could form only by intense star explosions called super nova. The earth and even our bodies and blood are so to speak, "star dust" from such an explosion. Earth could be made into its present form only after billions of years of "history" of the universe.

This billions of years' history was an unknown mystery to those who told, heard, wrote or read this Genesis text, for millennia of human experience. The text does convey an awareness of the mystery, but it doesn't make sense for God to try to convey the scientific story, before the knowledge base for science had been developed through many ages of human inquiry. God seems to expect and respect the human need to learn about nature through personal experience and shared knowledge.

There is yet another element in verse two of Genesis 1, stated by the words "...while a wind of God swept over the face of the waters." This suggests something of God's interaction with the yet not-fully formed substance of earth. The NRSV translation admits ambiguity about this interaction. The alternate readings are "...while the Spirit of God or while a mighty wind..." "...swept over the face of the waters."

To some ancient peoples, water represents the unknown boundaries of earth. Was God in some way dealing with these boundaries to form the earth? Science is at an utter loss to help us understand this interaction with God because God as a spiritual being cannot be weighed, measured or seen. Nor is God acknowledged by science as the direct or immediate cause of change.

Science, which is limited to observation of immediate cause, helps produce testable data and avoid wild speculation. A simple illustration might help us understand this. A mechanic studies and analyzes the mechanical components of a car to determine how they function. The mechanic may test drive the car along a road, around several corners and into a parking lot. He would note how the brakes are working, whether the steering wheel functions easily without a wobble in its connection to the wheels, how the engine accelerates and idles, and whether the turn signals and lights work properly. After returning from the test drive, the mechanic could tell the car owner whether the car is functioning well, whether the brakes need to be replaced, or the engine needs to be tuned. What the mechanic did to test the car would be a scientific engineering study of immediate causes related to the mechanical parts of the car.

An ultimate result of the test drive is that the mechanic is paid by the owner for his inspection and any necessary repair work. The owner might take the same drive to the parking lot, causing the parts of the car to function much as the mechanic did, but the owner's ultimate reason for the drive was to get a cup of cappuccino at a shop next to the parking lot. The driver's desire for a cappuccino and the mechanic's desire to be paid result in similar functioning of the car, but their minds' processes are not part of the scientific study of the car's functioning. The mechanic's need to be paid and the owner's desire for a cappuccino are the ultimate causation for the drive, not a physically measurable thing.

The intent of the biblical text is different from the normal intent of science. This results in a lot of misunderstandings between those who read the text of Genesis, and mistakenly try to turn it into scientific pronouncements, and those who come to the text from a study of science or denying the validity of scientific pronouncements.

Verse two assures us that God has ultimate control and causation of the processes whereby the earth was formed. But the text is not an attempt to describe those immediate scientific causes in detail for the reader to test in the laboratory. We may draw a theological conclusion, not a scientific conclusion, about the meaning of the text.

Genesis gives evidence that God is revealing, in a relational way, God's own character as Creator, but that God allows humans the experience through science of finding the processes of nature which are ultimately guided by God's hidden hand.

An Important but Limited Role for Science

Astronomy, astrophysics and geology all contribute to our scientific understanding of how the solar system with its planets came to be. More specifically, they show how Planet Earth developed and became a habitat for living things, including humans. Our earth developed in the most recent one-third of the history of the universe.

The early universe could not have produced a planetary body with its rich chemical diversity like the earth, because it lacked elements with atomic weights of iron or higher. The big bang produced mostly the very lightweight and simple elements such as hydrogen and helium, which became the primary composition of the first stars. As part of the evolutionary development of those first stars, they had to explode as super novae in their final days in order to create the heaver elements of the periodic chart of chemical elements. The sun is a second-generation star that may live another 10 billion years or so. A habitable earth will likely not witness the death of our central star, but if properly cared for, it may be habitable for many millions or even billions of years. Science is unable to tell us what will happen to human beings. In our present form, our existence is quite fragile.

In the next chapter, we will explore what God is up to in addressing the mess that is to become a home for humans, and more importantly, according to John Walton, become a temple for God.

In the Beginning God Created

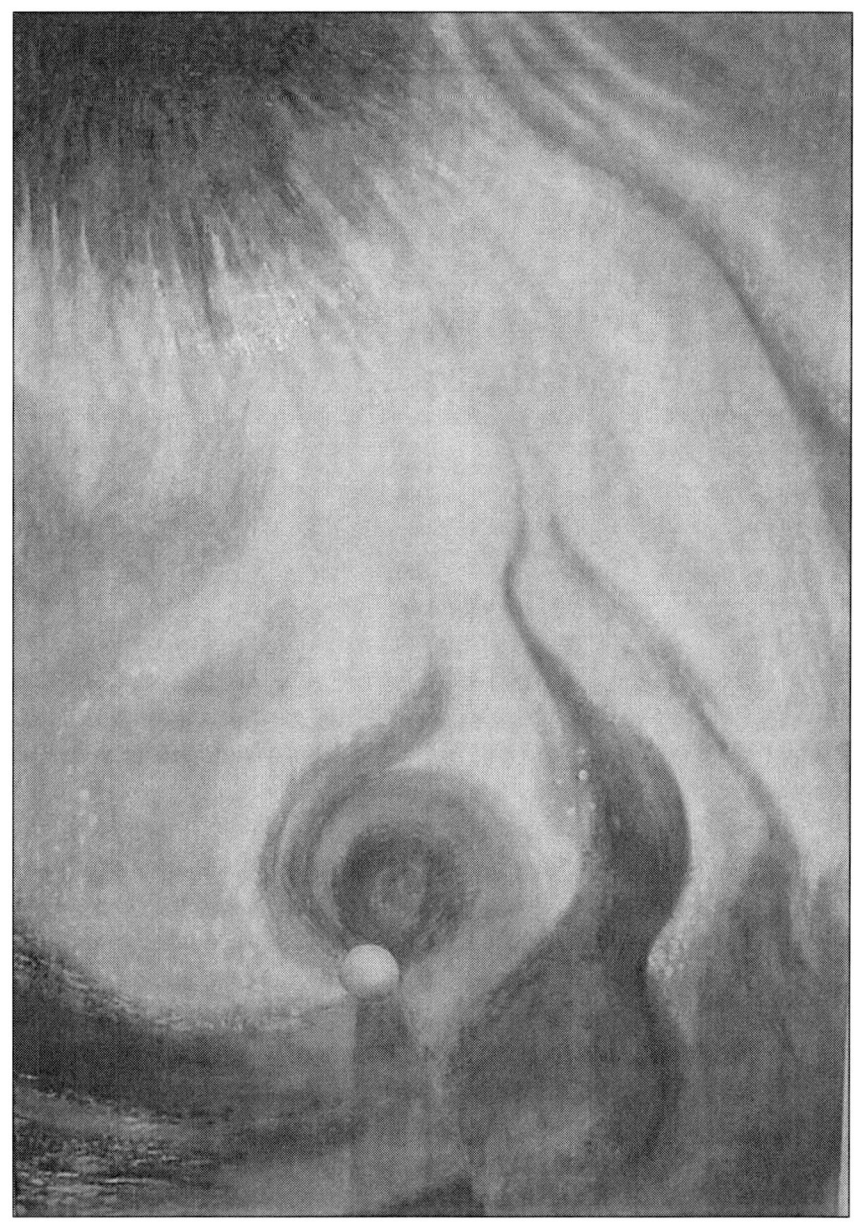

Creation Series, this one by Ruby Wiebe

Chapter 3

The Functions of Time, Weather and Food

(Days One to Three)

We continue in Genesis 1: 3-5 to see some of the functions that God created in order to prepare the earth for its inhabitants. Remember that these are basic functions that would make sense to the ancient Hebrews.

> "And God said, "Let there be light: and there was light. And God saw the light, that it was good: and God divided the light from the darkness. And God called the light Day, and the darkness he called Night. And the evening and the morning were the first day." (KJV)

> "God said, 'Let there be light'; and there was light. God saw that the light was good, and God separated the light from the darkness. God called the light Day, and the darkness He called Night. And there was evening and there was morning, a first day." (SJB)

> "Then God said, 'Let there be light'; and there was light. And God saw that the light was good; and God separated the light from the darkness. God called the light Day, and the darkness he called Night. And there was evening and there was morning, the first day. (NRSV)

"And God said, "Let there be light," and there was light. God saw that the light was good, and he separated the light from the darkness. God called the light "day," and the darkness he called "night." And there was evening, and there was morning—the first day. (NIV)

Let There Be Light (Day One)

The earth, as we know it, was not yet formed in verse 3, so the activity of God in speaking light into existence must be from a wider perspective than that of earth or its supposed boundary waters. Some commentators say that light without the sun being formed is nonsense. Such a view is a limited earthbound perspective. Science tells us that much of the light of the universe radiates from its stars. Our sun is a somewhat average second-generation star in the unfolding universe. Light came long before the earth and the sun we know today. Light, or more generally radiant energy, even had an intriguing roll in the 'Big Bang' universe, before any stars were formed. Science can tell us much about light, but does not explain how the speech of God formed light, or how God separated light from darkness.

Bodies like the earth and moon, space dust, and other dark matter of the universe cast their shadows, forming darkness by blocking the path of light's radiance. It is night, so to speak, in these dark shadows, but it is day in the radiance of light. These conditions could be named and understood long before science explained the rotation of the earth on its axis, providing periods of day and night on earth. The text reveals God as the ultimate source of this phenomenon of light and darkness, day and night, which provides the function of time for human beings.

But let's return to the intriguing statement that "God said", which is repeated throughout the first chapter of Genesis in a formulaic way. Human speech is a complex series of vibrations of our vocal cords that form sound waves carried through the medium of air to listeners. Most interpreters of the repeated statement of "God said" would not be so literalistic as to think that God was standing in earth's atmosphere, producing sound waves in the air.

We know that our own speech can be converted to many different media: squiggles on vinyl records, electromagnetic media, varying light tracks on compact disks, etc. There are dual capacities of encoding and decoding to produce an intelligible message. We have then the abstract idea of communication of information, which is what we humans understand to be the purpose of speech.

Thinking of God communicating information in creating the world is a powerful concept. In chapter three of *Belief in God in an Age of Science,* the author, John Polkinghorne, a scientist, suggests that God's providential interaction with creation is purely through top-down input of information. Science indicates the possibility of a world stranger and more exciting than the one imagined by Newton. There is the possibility of causality through information (the influence that brings about the formation of a structured pattern of future dynamical behavior.)

Our universe is a system of becoming. Polkinghorne gives five theological consequences of this idea. 1) The Creator need not be only the primary cause or just a physical interventionist, but the source of continuous active information. 2) If providence works in the unpredictabilities of physical process, it will be veiled from human view. 3) There are predictable aspects of the natural process that divine consistency maintains as signs of God's faithfulness. 4) There is both the possibility of God acting consistently in comparable circumstances, and of God acting in unprecedented and novel ways in other circumstances. 5) God may not know the future, for the future is not yet there to be known. "Involved in the act of creation, in the letting-be of the truly other, is not only a *kenosis* [Greek for emptying] of divine power, but also a *kenosis* of divine knowledge. Omniscience is self-limited by God in the creation of an open world of becoming."[26]

In his book *The Hidden Face of God,* the scientist author Gerald Schroeder also sees information or wisdom as essential to God's action in creation. His thesis is that the Creator is known through information or wisdom revealed in the universe. This is not knowledge in the sense of scientific proof, but an intimation of the hidden face of God. This is a valid thesis, but Genesis begins the personal revelation of God essential for faith that leads to a personal relationship with God. The nature of this personal relationship is described in the rest of the Hebrew Bible, and continues in the Greek addition to the Bible accepted by Christians. God's speaking functions of creation into existence and form is a non-intuitive revelation about God.

After God speaks day and night into existence, the text says "And there was evening and there was morning, the first day." But what kind of a day was this? From whose perspective are we to consider a day? We think of morning, noon, evening and night making a complete day cycle, but this text says evening first, then morning. "Probably the mention of the evening before morning reflects the Jewish concept that the day begins at dusk, not dawn. . . .In this view, the first day began in darkness (absence of light) (v 2) and ended after the creation of light, with nightfall, the start of the second day." [27]

We recognize that the oldest texts of Genesis in Hebrew are certainly Jewish, so we can expect their perspective. This does not answer whether this is the perspective of the original audience or what our perspective or even God's perspective is. The larger scope of this text moves through a whole creation week and ends in a Sabbath day of rest. Some see this as coming from the priestly tradition. John Walton sees these days as the creation of functions, which could take place in a 24-hour day. Another scholar, Derek Kidner, in *Genesis, An Introduction and Commentary,* has the following to say about the use of the word day in a seven-day week:

"To a modern reader, this at once raises the question of scientific accuracy. One may argue that 'day' can bear the sense of 'epoch' (*cf., e.g.*, Ps. 90:4; Is. 4:2), or that the days of God have no human analogies (as Augustine, and Origen before him, urged); others will take the days literally and find proof of human fallibility. . . .The assumption common to these interpretations is that God would not have us picture the creation as compressed into a mere week. But this may be exactly what God does intend us to do."[28]

As a teacher, I often had to simplify scientific concepts until my students' knowledge progressed to a higher level of understanding. "A God who made no concessions to our ways of seeing and of speaking would communicate to us no meaning. . . .It is only pedantry that would quarrel with terms that simplify in order to clarify."[29] Fretheim sees this as drawing us into a larger study.

The Genesis texts are prescientific in that they predate modern science, but not in the sense of having no interest in questions about causality. Israel's thinkers were very interested in the 'how' of creation, and not just questions of 'who' and 'why'. They recognized that truth about creation is not generated simply by theological reflection. We require various fields of inquiry in order to speak the full truth about the world. The task becomes one of integrating materials from various studies into a coherent statement about created order. In effect, Genesis invites every generation to be engaged in this process.[30]

Simplifying in order to clarify is the task I am attempting to do for you, the reader. But neither I, nor most readers, can plumb the full depth of knowledge that comes from Biblical theology or the scientific disciplines. What we can achieve is a greater appreciation for the Creator of it all, and thankfulness for our minds to probe even deeper into the realities of Word and world.

There are many different lengths of days in the universe. Earth's day has been changing over the vast scope of time since its creation. The first persons to receive this creation story, and those who have most recently joined the audience, find themselves on a journey to new perspectives. What is a day to us? Certainly our day is an opportunity to learn about God's world, and worship its Creator. God asserts his own evaluation of this first day's work by stating that light is good.

Science knows that light has a dual nature. Sometimes it behaves like electromagnetic waves, and sometimes it behaves like particles we call photons. This knowledge would be strange to our ancient Hebrews. John Walton assures us that the Genesis text is really talking about the function of light and of its absence, which we call darkness. These two, light and darkness, result in our understanding of time summarized as a day. The text is not discussing the creation of a material thing, but is talking about a day described in the old Hebrew sense as evening and morning. It can best be understood, in our terms, as the function of time. To the ancient people, the function of time was caused by the rising and setting of the sun, and the appearance of the moon at night. We still use terms like rising and setting, but we know it results from the rotation of the earth. The changes of the moon's appearance or phases result from the moon revolving about the earth, and both revolving around the sun. These are different perspectives, not a basis for arguments about truth or fiction.

What we moderns scientifically call light would have existed in the early universe billions of years before many of the chemical elements found on earth, as we know it. The earth itself would have begun to form in a cloud of gas and dust that were left over remnants from one or more previous, dying star, explosions. The central and largest accumulating mass of this cloud would eventually become a new star, our sun. Other accumulating masses in the cloud formed the earth and its sister planets of our solar system.

The early earth was likely a violently changing place, with powerful storms and lighter gases being swept from its atmosphere by solar winds. As the forming sun condensed sufficiently to ignite the nuclear fusion of hydrogen, light began shining brightly on the earth, in addition to the light of distant stars, perhaps obscured on the earth's surface by the density of the early atmosphere. At some point, due to the rotation of the earth, day and night could become reality, if an observer would have been present. However, this would have been long before an earthling, or even any other animal, lived on the earth. Time was a significant function, created by God on the first day of creation, as described in the text of Genesis.

God and Time

How would we live without time? What does time mean to God? Theology describes God as eternal. We humans pack our schedules full with periods of time we often divide down to hours and minutes. If we are observing sporting events, even seconds or tenths of seconds become important. In the scientific arena, such as a description of the big bang, even milliseconds become important for subatomic and atomic events. Some of us may often feel like slaves of time, but rejoice in free time. We buy and sell time as though it were a commodity. An entire theological treatise could be written on our use of time. Perhaps God is dismayed when he sees how we humans use our time. But let's stop here.

The God of Creation and Word

There is another theological topic in relation to the God of Creation. For Christians, the Gospel of John starts with another important characterization of God. John 1:1-5 reads in the NRSV:

"In the beginning was the Word, and the Word was with God, and the Word was God. 2 He was in the beginning with God. 3 All things came into being through him, and without him not one thing came into being. What has come into being 4 in him was life, and the life was the light of all people. 5 The light shines in the darkness, and the darkness did not overcome it."

This highly theological formulation leaves some atheistic scientists as muddled as many Christians feel when nuclear physicists use the jargon of advanced mathematics in describing the big bang creation of the universe. We can be thankful to God for both our scientists and our theologians – after all, God created both, and God understands the language both are using.

Genesis suggests that God communicated when God said, "Let there be light." The gospel of John calls this creator God, the Word. God is the original communicator. Christians understand this Word to be Jesus Christ, who came in human form to communicate God to us who live on the functional earth God spoke to create.

The gospel of John has another striking theological idea related to light. What God was bringing into being was life, which was the light of all people. It takes words or light for us to see the full picture. We use all kinds of metaphors to communicate or make sense of our lives, to become enlightened. We need to respect the light of our God-like humanness as we follow distinctly different paths in fulfilling our lives. However, we should all be able to agree with God's declaration "that the light was good!"

Bible believers from many different perspectives have argued with each other as to whether the days of Genesis were 24 hours, or long periods of time. If the Genesis day is to be thought of as a period of 24 hours, all the scientific evidence of the development of earth and its living things must be illusions, they assert. The days must have miraculous processes, which some would rather describe as magical illusions. If we take John Walton's viewpoint, then God created functions and set up functionaries in each of six 24-hour days that were worked out in material form over the eons of geologic time.

But of course, we could also take these creation days metaphorically, as being God's time. Even scripture says: Ps 90:4 "For a thousand years in your sight are like yesterday when it is past, or like a watch in the night." (NRSV) "4 For a thousand years in your sight are like a day that has just gone by, or like a watch in the night." (NIV) This verse is not a mathematical ratio of a thousand to one between a human day and a God day, but it tells us that God is not bound by time in the way that we are. A Genesis day could be whatever time is needed for a scientific description of the creation of earth. In either case, the Genesis days of creation are no basis for an argument of merit between science and scripture.

Let the Earth Have Sky (Day Two)

We come to Day Two, in Genesis 1:6-8, and it deals with a metaphoric image that puzzled ancient peoples as they tried to imagine a mechanism for the function that permitted water to fall out of the sky.

> "And God said, 'Let there be a firmament in the midst of the waters, and let it divide the waters from the waters.' And God made the firmament, and divided the waters that were under the firmament from the waters that were above the firmament: and it was so. And God called the firmament Heaven. And the evening and the morning were the second day." (KJV)

> "God said, 'let there be an expanse in the midst of the water, that it might separate water from water.' God made the expanse, and it separated the water that was below the expanse from the water that was above the expanse. And it was so. God called the expanse sky. And there was evening and there was morning, a second day." (SJB)

"And God said, 'Let there be a dome in the midst of the waters, and let it separate the waters from the waters.' So God made the dome and separated the waters that were under the dome from the waters that were above the dome. And it was so. God called the dome Sky. And there was evening and there was morning, the second day." (NRSV)

"And God said, 'Let there be an expanse between the waters to separate water from water.' So God made the expanse and separated the water under the expanse from the water above it. And it was so. God called the expanse "sky." And there was evening, and there was morning—the second day." (NIV)

To the scientifically primitive observer, water and ice coming down out of God's "sky" was a mystery. What held the water and ice up in the first place? In Job 38, God's answer to Job seems to taunt Job with these perplexing questions. "Have you entered the storehouses of the snow, or have you seen the storehouses of the hail. . .? . . .Has the rain a father, or who has begotten the drops of dew? From whose womb did the ice come forth, and who gave birth to the hoarfrost of heaven? . . .Who has the wisdom to number the clouds? Or who can tilt the water skins of the heavens, when the dust runs into a mass and the clods cling together?" The wise preacher of Ecclesiastes observed: "When clouds are full, they empty rain on the earth;" (Ecl.11:3a.) And God also noted: "All streams run to the sea, but the sea is not full; to the place where the streams flow, there they continue to flow." (Ecl.1:7) The relationship of water to the sky and to the streams of the earth was a mystery to the early Genesis audience, as well as the more highly sophisticated readers in the advanced culture of Israel.

Any high school student who has studied some basic meteorology and knows something of the hydrological cycle could answer these questions. We know there is no beaten metal or crystal dome in the sky holding up the water. We know the sky to be the air or atmosphere of gases that surround our planet earth. Clouds are flotsam and jetsam of water droplets or ice crystals adrift in the sea of air, but we don't think of them as giant water balloons filling until they burst out with rain.

It is important not be over-literalistic in our reading of this or the rest of the creation story. While the creation story touches on scientific knowledge, it does not have the last word as to the physical structures of nature. Certainly, the creation story communicates that God created the sky, in whatever terms the audience might use to describe it.

Formation of the atmosphere to sustain and protect life and water the earth is an important part of the geologic history of our earth. Some 4.6 billion years ago, the earth's crust began to solidify as it cooled down from its hot molten state. The crust formed the first igneous rocks whose age we can measure by radioactive isotopes.

On the early earth, the atmosphere was extremely hostile to life, as we know it. There must have been very violent electrical storms and hot, caustic rains. Within a billion years or less, the atmosphere had changed enough so that living things could survive.[31] Early life itself transformed the atmosphere to an oxygen-rich mix able to sustain complex creatures.[32] We can read the story of the atmosphere in the sedimentary rocks. It is a story that spans over four billion years, and still goes on today.

Our species is adding to the current chapter of the composition of the atmosphere with its air pollution, adding greenhouse gases, with the likelihood of global warming. The story of the development of our atmosphere is a worthy story for the evening and the morning of God's second creative day. We need to play a more responsible part in its history. Interestingly, the Genesis text seems to have forgotten to note that God's work in making the sky was good. Perhaps this part of creation is left in our hands to make it "good."

Science is teaching us that the earth, viewed by pre-scientific people as endless, is actually a quite limited home. The earth is only a small planet in its own solar system. The dominant sun of this system is an insignificant star on the outer reaches of the Milky Way galaxy, which is only one of billions of galaxies. However, this tiny speck in the universe is the home of the only organic life we have been able to identify, although there could be more. This is the life we humans experience here and now.

If we want life, as we know it, to continue for future generations, we must care for this speck of earth and its life-supporting "dome" of atmosphere. "Even with only moderate global warming, possible effects will be noted in food production (especially if increased desertification occurs in the continental land mass of the Northern Hemisphere), shifting zones of forestation/deforestation, and rising sea levels. These moderate effects will have an immoderate influence on human health, global food supplies, and weather patterns. It follows that an altered lifestyle must be undertaken and soon."[33] Will what we do to our atmosphere be "good?"

The importance of water

In early Jewish culture, most people had to carry water to their homes in a variety of containers. It was a mystery to them how the water that came down as rain was apparently held in some magical container up in the sky. Some imagined a container made from a kind of solid crystalline material, because they could see the sun, moon and stars through it. They did associate clouds with rain, but apparently clouds did not seem substantial enough to them to carry rain.

The KJV calls the sky, "firmament," carrying some of this ancient Hebrew idea. SJB and NIV make more of an acknowledgment of modern readers' expectations by simply calling it an expanse. The idea of expanse is also a very old one, and may have represented what the writer of Genesis had in mind. But the NRSV may be closer to the ancient understanding by using the term "dome," which suggests shape, more than composition. The importance of access to water for ancient people is reflected in the Genesis verses that say that God created rainwater as separate from the water carried by the solid surface of the earth as seas, lakes and rivers. We know that it is really the clouds that carry rain. The overall function resulting from separating water below from water above, whether it's separated by a firmament, expanse, or dome, is the weather.

We know that in addition to solid and liquids, there are gasses, and water can be in all three of those forms. To the ancient people, the concept of water as solid, liquid and gas (ice, water and steam) would have been as mysterious as non-Christians trying to understand the Christian concept of God as Father, Son, and Holy Spirit. We think of gaseous water as being part of the earth's atmosphere, but unless we have a scientific bent or were made to study it in a science course, we may never have seriously considered how clouds really function in bringing rain.

Let's take a brief, simplified tour of the function of rain God created. Rain and water are as essential to our wellbeing as food, as pain to injuries. Clouds usually are formed, in part, of very tiny particles carried by updrafts in the air. As clouds rise, they cool and some of the gaseous water condenses on the surface of the cloud particles. If sufficient water is present, these droplets can grow in size. They may also collide with one another, sticking together as larger drops. Eventually the drops may become large enough as to no longer be supported in the cloud updraft, but to fall as rain.

Let's do a little mathematical analysis of the situation. Let's say, we have a cloud stretching over one hundred square miles of our landscape. Perhaps the cloud extends a mile upward from its base to its upper surface. Let's say it rains 12 inches, or a foot, of water over several hours on this area of one hundred square miles. If the rain didn't soak in to the earth, there would be a flood a foot deep on a flat surface. If the same rain ran down into a ten-square mile valley, the flood would become ten foot deep. If it then also gained speed, traveling down stream channels as a wall of water ten feet high sweeping away houses and other structures, it could cause millions of dollars of damage. Whew!

But how much water was the cloud carrying per cubic foot? An original one-cubic foot of water on the flat land surface would take up 5,280 cubic feet of space above it in the cloud. So one cubic foot of water is spread over 5,280 cubic feet of cloud. A cubic foot of water weighs about 64 pounds, and a pint of water weighs about a pound. So there are 64 pints of water spread over 5,280 cubic feet of cloud. Each cubic foot of cloud has only 64 pints divided by 5,280. This is roughly a ratio of 6/500 or 12/1000 or 1.2 pints per 100 cubic feet of cloud, which is the same as .012 pints in a cubic foot of cloud. In God's creation, this function of a cloud does not require a massive crystalline firmament dome to support water to be dropped from a window as rain on the earth.

How about explaining gravity, or the van der Waals forces that bind water into rain droplets? I could go on and on about all that is involved in making God's function of rain work.

According to Wikipedia, "The van der Waals equation is an equation of state for a fluid composed of particles that have a non-zero volume and a pairwise attractive inter-particle force (such as the van der Waals force). It was derived in 1873 by Johannes Diderik van der Waals, who received the Nobel Prize in 1910 for his work on the equation of state for gases and liquids. The equation is based on a modification of the ideal gas law and approximates the behavior of real fluids, taking into account the nonzero size of molecules and the attraction between them."

Aren't you glad the Bible didn't try to be scientific when it mentions creation of the function that makes rain? There would be many other functions that Genesis would need to articulate if it were trying to say something about the science of rain. I won't bother to give you the equation, but I will assure you that God knew what God was doing by creating the function of rain, and what the inspired writers of scripture should and should not report.

Rain and weather were important to the creation of human beings, Adam and Eve, from the dust of the earth. On day three, God created another function essential for human life.

Let the Earth Have Seas and Dry Land (Day Three, Step 1)

There are two separate steps in creating the function of food on day three. The first step in Gen 1:9-10 is separating the land from water, in preparation for growing food.

> "And God said, 'Let the waters under the heaven be gathered together unto one place, and let the dry land appear:' and it was so. And God called the dry land Earth; and the gathering together of the waters called He Seas: and God saw that it was good." (KJV)

> "God said, 'Let the water below the sky be gathered into one area, that the dry land may appear.' And it was so. God called the dry

land Earth, and the gathering of waters He called Seas. And God saw that this was good." (SJB)

"And God said, 'Let the waters under the sky be gathered together into one place, and let the dry land appear.' And it was so. God called the dry land Earth, and the waters that were gathered together he called Seas. And God saw that it was good." (NRSV)

"And God said, 'Let the water under the sky be gathered to one place, and let dry ground appear.' And it was so. God called the dry ground "land," and the gathered waters he called "seas." And God saw that it was good." (NIV)

Take a look at a globe. It distinguishes water from land, and you will see that the surface our planet is more water than land. You may remember that water covers about three-fourths of our earth's surface. What you may not know is that if the surface of the solid material of earth were of equal elevation, water would cover all the land to a depth of several miles. An extraterrestrial observer might think that our planet is composed of water—one big drop of water. Ha! Perhaps this is what it looked like in an early stage of earth history. Since we humans are land dwellers, there would be no human beings. The most intelligent creatures on earth would perhaps be some kind of fish, though not whales. Whales appear to be land dwellers that returned to the sea.

At this stage of creation, now already day three, it is again noted that God observed that "it was good." I, along with the ancient Hebrew readers, agree with God's observation. The depth of the sea was a fearful thing. Note that Jonah's punishment for trying to get away from God was to be thrown into the terrifying, stormy sea. He had probably taken this route because to ancient peoples, the sea was often looked upon as a dwelling place for evil, the last place you would expect God to be.

Making part of the surface of the earth to be land was a "good" thing. Fishermen and seafarers would have also known good aspects of the sea. Divers return to us land dwellers wonderful pictures of seascapes and sea dwelling life which we enjoy and at which we marvel. Indeed, both land and sea, being separated, makes our planetary home a more wonderful place to provide for our lives.

Scientifically, separation of land and sea is possible because the earth has a more complicated structure than just that of a big drop of water or a simple ball of minerals. The earth has a solid rocky surface, a somewhat plastic and flexible middle layer, and a hot molten core. The rocks have a variety of mineral compositions and densities. Hot molten rock lavas tend to push upward, and the lighter density rocks tend to reach higher elevations than denser rocks. While this is a great oversimplification of what happens geologically, these are basic structural conditions and processes that allow some rocky materials to make mountains and others ocean basins or valleys for rivers and lakes. The diverse landscapes and seascapes add beauty to our world. Thank you God!

The geologic story related to this creative act is a drama that has been clarified through a significant paradigm shift during my lifetime. We now understand that the outer rigid crust of the earth is divided into separate plates, much like pans of ice in the sea or river after a spring thaw. They float on denser, more elastic rock layers beneath them. These layers move, causing the plate edges to collide and push over or under each other, buckling and partially melting, to form mountains and volcanoes. The dry land or continents are the lighter granitic rocks of the plates that rise the most in elevation, while denser, basaltic plate rocks form the ocean basins. These differences of elevation allow water to collect in seas and dry land to appear on the continents.

This drama has continued from the first solidification of crust 4.6 billion years ago to present events of earthquakes and volcanoes. Continents have drifted over the face of the earth, at times colliding to form supercontinents, with widely-spread common forms of life, at other times separating to form smaller island continents like Australia, with its distinct creatures.[34] India has been and continues to collide with the great Asian landmass to form earth's highest mountains. The story of life is tied to these changing landforms. God again saw that it was "good." Humans may never be able to tamper with this system.

Let the Land Produce Plants (Day Three, Step 2)

Day three is not complete, even though God has already pronounced it good. There is a greater overall function to be achieved by Step 2 on the third day, as described in Genesis 1:11-13:

> "And God said, 'Let the earth bring forth grass, the herb yielding seed, and the fruit tree yielding fruit after his kind, whose seed is in itself, upon the earth:' and it was so. And the earth brought forth grass and herb yielding seed after his kind, and the tree yielding fruit, whose seed was in itself, after his kind: and God saw that it was good. And the evening and the morning were the third day." (KJV)

> "And God said, 'Let the earth sprout vegetation: seed-bearing plants, fruit trees of every kind on earth that bear fruit with the seed in it.' And it was so. The earth brought forth vegetation: seed-bearing plants of every kind, and trees of every kind bearing fruit with the seed in it. And God saw that it was good. And there was evening and there was morning, a third day." (SJB)

> "Then God said, 'Let the earth put forth vegetation: plants yielding seed, and fruit trees of every kind on earth that bear fruit with the seed in it.' And it was so. The earth brought forth vegetation: plants yielding seed of every kind, and trees of every kind bearing fruit with the seed in it. And God saw that it was good. And there was evening and there was morning, the third day." (NRSV)

> "Then God said,' Let the land produce vegetation: seed-bearing plants and trees on the land that bear fruit with seed in it, according to their various kinds.' And it was so. The land produced vegetation: plants bearing seed according to their kinds and trees bearing fruit with seed in it according to their kinds. And God saw that it was good. And there was evening, and there was morning—the third day." (NIV)

In the second speech of day three, God says to the land "Let the earth put forth vegetation". Then Genesis itemizes two or three kinds of reproducing vegetation. This rudimentary classification system has mushroomed into hundreds of thousands of categories developed by plant taxonomists. The vegetation described in Genesis is made up largely of plants providing food for earth's living things. The Genesis description is not a scientific list of every category of plants, the way biologists describe them. A scientific account of plants would not have made sense to most early readers of Genesis. It would have detracted from the main point about what God was doing. God was providing food for creatures yet to be created; somewhat similar to Joseph providing food for Egypt in the time of famine. This section of Genesis is preparing the reader for the creation of functionaries described in the next section of Genesis.

We now have land and water that are needed as functionaries bringing plants into existence at God's command. This is not the creation of plants out of nothing, but rather the development of plants out of materials found in water and in the soil. Plants, animals, and our own human bodies are made up of a large percentage of water. The remainder of plants, animals and human bodies consist of other components derived from the chemical elements found on land. There is nothing in this Genesis description that denies scientific attempts to show that living cells could arise from earth's materials, although science cannot say as Genesis does, that God is the Creator. Near Eastern cultural understanding of food crops include crops grown in water, the way in the Far East rice is grown on land covered by water.

We need both the Bible and science for a full understanding of the world in which we live. God's speech brought forth properties already inherent in the earth. The earth was created to develop living forms. There is no major impassible wall of distinction between inorganic and organic. Let the 'intelligent design' advocates beware of limiting our view of God's action as an unexplainable special creation of 'irreducible complexity' at the beginning of life. Rather, let us see God's stupendous acts of creation in the inorganic world of earth plates, as well as the continuing unfolding of the organic world of living things.

Seeds are a more recent addition to the plants' means of reproduction. Seed–bearing grasses, fruiting, and flowering plants are a more recent addition to the fossil record of multicellular plants. The earliest living plants and bacteria grew largely in the shallow seas, and appear in the sedimentary record as long as 3.5 billion years ago.[35] God's creation of vegetation has a long and distinguished history which paleontologists are beginning to read in the rocks. God likes this history as well, and has pronounced his handiwork as good, as a function to provide food.

What an astounding evening and morning on the third day of the creation of the world! This wraps up a distinct set of days in God's creative week, and is followed by another set of three days that show a parallel structure and related creative activity. There is more going on here than a simple six-day sequence in a week of work. Commentators have noted a tie between day one and day four. On day one, God says, "Let there be light," and on day four, God says, "Let there be lights."

Similarly, day two has a dome of sky and the separation of waters above and beneath it. Day five God prepares creatures to swim in the waters and to fly in the sky. Again, on day three, God separates the land from the water and prepares plants. On day six, God makes animals to live on the land (including the creation of humans), and provides that plants sustain these creatures as food.

What Is the Time of Creation?

A day/age theory that tries to force geologic periods into the days of Genesis is faulty in several ways. There is no simple relationship as defined by a ratio (*i.e.*, one creation day equals a thousand geologic years, is wide of the mark) for days to the duration of geologic periods. Nor does giving the perspective of God's time related to background radiation from the initial 'Big Bang' lead to sequential creation days.

Even if the whole six-day creation week were an accurate ratio to our own frame of reference, with its 14-billion year old universe, as Gerald Schroeder contends in his books,[36] we would still have a problem of the creation order among the days. Green plants would not thrive on the earth on the third day before the earth's sun is created on day four. In some ways, day four must be seen as contiguous with day one, with events before day two and three. Now of course, if evening four were only 12 hours of darkness before the sunlight shone on the plants of day three, there would be no problem, but we have already shown through science that the activities of any one day may have occurred over billions of years. I would contend that although 24-hour days and sequential numbering are God's simplified way of revelation to his pre-scientific people, we need not and should not be limited by such contrived, literalistic interpretation.

I find Wenham's comments in the quotation below helpful.

"It has been unfortunate that one device which our narrative uses to express the coherence and purposiveness of the creator's work, namely, the distribution of the various creative acts to six days, has been seized on and interpreted over-literalistically, with the result that science and Scripture have been pitted against each other instead of being seen as complementary. Properly understood, Genesis justifies the scientific experience of unity and order in nature. Other devices include the use of repeating formulae, the tendency to group words and phrases into tens and sevens, literary techniques such as chiasm and inclusio, the arrangement of creative acts into matching groups, and so on."[37]

It should be noted that early scientists, (often Christian), pursued their studies because of a strong sense of God's consistency and order in nature. Wenham sees this as required for science.

"Genesis 1 provided the underpinning of the scientific enterprise with the assumption that unity and order prevail because almighty God created and controls the world according to a coherent plan. This assumption can justify the experimental method. If the world were controlled by a multitude of capricious deities, or subject to mere chance, no consistency could be expected in experimental results and no scientific laws could be discovered.[38]"

In the approach taken by Walton, functions are created and authority is granted to functionaries in the six 24-hour days of creation. Compare this with how quickly the same process was done by Pharaoh, after Joseph interpreted Pharaoh's famine dreams. Whether the six days are about functions, or are a literary device not to be taken literally, they should not be used to pit scripture against science.

Time of Creation in Science and Scriptures

Since the origin of the "Big Bang" theory of the beginning of the universe, science has endeavored to set a time for the beginning of the universe. As of March 22, 2013, the current refinement of this came up with 13.77 billion years, with an uncertainty of only 0.4% for the "Big Bang" of when it all got started. According to the Wikipedia article on the Age of the universe, "the uncertainty of 37 million years has been obtained by the agreement of a number of scientific research projects, such as microwave background radiation measurements by the Planck satellite and other probes. Measurements of the cosmic background radiation give the cooling time of the universe since the Big Bang. Measurements of the expansion rate of the universe can be used to calculate its approximate age by extrapolating backwards in time." For many of us, this may have little meaning because we do not understand the theory and equations by which such calculations are made.

Age also relates to the present size of the universe since it is expanding. Stars exist in certain classes or categories related to how their nuclear furnaces function. Some always show a well-known brightness and wavelength of emitted light or radiant energy. This means that a dimmer-appearing star is further away in the universe. By measuring brightness, we can measure distance from us in the years that it took a star's light to reach us. The universe must be at least as old as the time it took a star's light to reach us. Astronomers and physicists have various measuring sticks they trust. For non-specialists, it takes a measure of faith, but due to the basis of the scientific method that relies on debate, evidence, and self-correction, it need not be blind faith.

Although the Bible states that in the beginning God created the heaven and the earth, it does not try to give us a time for the beginning. Some will dispute this by saying that creation took place in seven days, and that from Adam on we have genealogical records in years that take us back to a beginning of about 6,000 years ago. However, Genesis clearly says that the earth was without form and void and then proceeds to give functions that shape the earth with land, continents and sea, oceans with fish, heavens in which birds fly, the atmosphere as we call it and know it, and land animals including human beings. It makes sense to consider the earth in its present form a different age than the beginning of the universe, but the Bible does not tell us the amount of time between the beginning of the heaven and the beginning of the formed earth as we now know it. Science does give us this kind of a time measure. It indicates that the earth is about 4.5 billion years old, or only about one-third as old as the universe. There are many geologic measures for the age of different kinds of rocks; most related to the disintegration rates of different radioactive isotopes. Geologists have put together time scales related to the layers of earth rocks and fossils that sedimentary rocks contain. So we have knowledge of how old the earth is and its changing life forms.

Psalms 90 suggests to some Bible readers that God's time is in a ratio of 1,000 years to one day of human time. But this is better seen as similar to Jesus' reply when asked whether we should forgive seven times. Jesus told us to forgive seventy times seventy. Of course Jesus did not mean for us to count forgiving up to 490 times and then no longer forgive. Psalms 90 only suggests that the eternal God does not count time the way humans count time. For me, personally, I believe like J. B. Phillips, who has suggested "Your God Is Too Small." The God that I find in the created world as described by science gives me a greater appreciation for God's greatness and eternal nature.

In the text of this book I have suggested that we should not equate the creation of Adam and Eve with the creation of human beings in Genesis 1. Also I doubt that we can read the genealogies following the story of Adam and Eve, as we would track years in genealogies as we do at present. The purpose of these genealogies was not to date the time of creation. God has not given us a scientific document. A scientific document would not have made much sense in the years since the scriptures have existed. Rather, God has revealed God's self, so that we may relate to God on a personal basis. This is a far greater truth than scientific knowledge.

The Functions of Time, Weather and Food

Creation Series, this one by Stephen King

Chapter 4

Functionaries Installed

―⚒―

Let Sun, Moon and Stars Be Visible (Day Four)

Day four is described by Gen 1:14-19:

> "And God said, 'Let there be lights in the firmament of the heaven to divide the day from the night; and let them be for signs, and for seasons, and for days, and years: And let them be for lights in the firmament of the heaven to give light upon the earth: and it was so.' And God made two great lights; the greater light to rule the day, and the lesser light to rule the night: he made the stars also. And God set them in the firmament of the heaven to give light upon the earth, and to rule over the day and over the night, and to divide the light from the darkness: and God saw that it was good. 1And the evening and the morning were the fourth day." (KJV)

> "And God said, 'Let there be lights in the expanse of the sky to separate the day from the night; they shall serve as signs for the set times—the days and years; and they shall serve as lights in the expanse of the sky to shine upon the earth.' And it was so. God made the two great lights, the greater light to dominate the day and the lesser light to dominate the night, and the stars. God set them in the expanse of the sky to shine upon the earth, to dominate the day and the night, and to separate light from darkness. And

God saw that this was good. 1And there was evening, and there was morning, a fourth day." SJB

"And God said, 'Let there be lights in the dome of the sky to separate the day from the night; and let them be for signs and for seasons and for days and years, and let them be lights in the dome of the sky to give light upon the earth.' And it was so. God made the two great lights—the greater light to rule the day and the lesser light to rule the night— and the stars. God set them in the dome of the sky to give light upon the earth, to rule over the day and over the night, and to separate the light from the darkness. And God saw that it was good. And there was evening and there was morning, the fourth day." NRSV

"And God said, 'Let there be lights in the expanse of the sky to separate the day from the night, and let them serve as signs to mark seasons and days and years, and let them be lights in the expanse of the sky to give light on the earth.' And it was so. God made two great lights—the greater light to govern the day and the lesser light to govern the night. He also made the stars. God set them in the expanse of the sky to give light on the earth, to govern the day and the night, and to separate light from darkness. And God saw that it was good. And there was evening, and there was morning—the fourth day." NIV

If we continue with Walton's understanding of ancient myths, we now have God setting up functionaries, just as Pharaoh told Joseph to appoint officers over Egypt to collect grain. Of course, God was also the Creator of the physical objects of the astronomical bodies. But all that needs to be done in the time of day four is to assign functionaries, similar to the way Joseph appointed officers to collect grain.

    The heavenly lights provided a working basis for signs and seasons, days and years. Even an audience with rudimentary astronomical knowledge has a culture that defines different time intervals, dependent on the changing appearance of heavenly bodies. Many cultures have elevated the mystery of these objects into a pantheon of deities. God's speech should be heard as countering such false human imaginations. Note, how according to Wenham, the Hebrew wording denies the existence of deities other than the God of the Hebrews.

"First the sun, moon, and stars are created by God: they are creatures not gods. . . .Second, the sun and moon are not given their usual Hebrew names, which might suggest identification with Shamash the sun god, or Yar the moon god. Instead they are simply called 'the larger' and 'the smaller light.' Third, the sun and moon are simply assigned the role of lighting the earth and ruling the day and the night, as surrogates of God. . . .Finally, the stars, widely worshiped and often regarded as controllers of human destiny, are mentioned almost as an afterthought: they, too, are merely creatures."[39]

This, too, God saw as good. One additional comment may be needed here. We humans can have such pendulum swings in our attitudes. These days, sun, moon, and stars receive little homage as gods among us, but perhaps we are beginning to downgrade them as objects for our exploration and use. We have already visited the moon, with mixed utilitarian results. It is really only an earth sister in a dual planetary system. We are a long way from exploiting, in person; the resource of the moon, which in reality is material quite like earth and perhaps in the past was even one body with the earth.[40] The moon is a mere 240,000 miles away, while the sun is 93 million miles away, though only $8^1/_2$ light minutes.

A round trip to any other star or its planetary system would require a significant part of a human lifetime, or more likely many generations, even if travel speeds could reach a significant percentage of the speed of light. Could you imagine descendants of 20 generations after Columbus's crew left Europe, returning to report? Europeans would just now begin learning about the 'new world' over the horizon of the ocean. Think about the problems the returning crew might have, finding and reporting to the descendants of those who sent them. We can look billions of light years out into the heavens, but we are really quite earthbound creatures, and will continue to be in our present physical bodies.

A triumph of astronomical science, which we almost take for granted today, was the realization that "our" sun is just a star. Put in the converse, the stars are really much like our sun, but at immense distances from us. More recently, we have learned that stars, the sun included, are nuclear fusion furnaces that are born, and then die. When our sun dies, life on earth is expected to die. But don't worry yet—that is billions of years in the future. I have not told much of the scientific story of stars, but it is well worth studying.

Stars and Their Energy

On the topic of energy use or conservation, most stars emit more energy in a few minutes than humans have used since the beginning of creation. This energy is simply dispersed into space. God appears to easily bankroll all this energy and this for the glory of God, or so I think, as I perceive the hidden hand of God in the fourth day of creation. There is much in the structure and composition of the universe that I have not touched on and that is not mentioned in our Genesis account. It, too, illuminates the hidden hand of God.

The Hebrew Scriptures have these celestial objects correctly related to the function of time in a parallel to light and dark of day one. The sun provides day, and its setting (rotation of the earth away from the sun) provides night. The phases of the moon (the result of its orbit around earth changing its position relative to the sun) provide for months. A year results from the changing skyscape of stars as the earth moves in its orbit around the sun.

I have described this all according to the heliocentric view, not according to the geocentric view that corresponds to the language of the Bible. This major change of perspective is one most of us would agree does not alter the reliability of scripture. We now need to face another major change of perspective accepting our relatedness to the other creatures of the earth, and to the changes in living creatures that the fossil records clearly shows. This relatedness also will not be a threat to the reliability of scripture.

Let the Water Swarm with Aquatic Life (Day Five)

Day five, Gen 1:20-23, is a scene of high productivity.

"And God said, 'Let the waters bring forth abundantly the moving creature that hath life, and fowl that may fly above the earth in the open firmament of heaven.' And God created great whales, and every living creature that moveth, which the waters brought forth abundantly, after their kind, and every winged fowl after his kind: and God saw that it was good. And God blessed them, saying, Be fruitful, and multiply, and fill the waters in the seas, and let fowl multiply in the earth. And the evening and the morning were the fifth day." (KJV)

"God Said, 'Let the waters bring forth swarms of living creatures, and birds that fly above the earth across the expanse of the sky.' God created the great sea monsters and all the living creatures of every kind that creep, which the waters brought forth in swarms, and all the winged birds of every kind. And God saw that this was good. 22 God blessed them, saying 'Be fertile and increase, fill the waters in the seas, and let the birds increase on the earth.' And there was evening and there was morning, a fifth day." (SJB)

"And God said, 'Let the waters bring forth swarms of living creatures, and let birds fly above the earth across the dome of the sky.' So God created the great sea monsters and every living creature that moves, of every kind, with which the waters swarm, and every winged bird of every kind. And God saw that it was good. God blessed them, saying, "Be fruitful and multiply and fill the waters in the seas, and let birds multiply on the earth." And there was evening and there was morning, the fifth day." (NRSV)

"And God said, 'Let the water teem with living creatures, and let birds fly above the earth across the expanse of the sky.' So God created the great creatures of the sea and every living and moving thing with which the water teems, according to their kinds, and every winged bird according to its kind. And God saw that it was good. God blessed them and said, "Be fruitful and increase in number and fill the water in the seas, and let the birds increase on the earth." And there was evening, and there was morning—the fifth day." (NIV)

Here again, we hear God speaking to a medium—water in this case, which he endows with the ability to bring forth living things. This is certainly not a creation out of nothing by a magical snap of God's fingers. For several decades now, but still in a rudimentary way, science has been able to say something about this mechanism. Beware though, of positing an irreducible, intelligent design requirement! Science, as now structured, will ever and only find and give natural mechanisms for this beginning of life in water. This does not say that there is no intelligent design. The more we learn about this mechanism, the more intelligent it appears to be. The scripture affirms God's hidden hand or spoken word in all creation, including organisms living in water, whether one-celled or whale-sized "sea monsters."

Sea monsters may have grabbed the imagination of primitive peoples, but things too small for the eye to see have stimulated scientific imagination. We are becoming aware of the molecular level, biochemical mechanisms, that are the basis for all life on earth. This life in water also converges with the life of plants. Our age needs to face the challenges related to creation and evolution.

Created by Chance or Divine Intention?

Darwin, a naturalist *par excellence*, sought a natural mechanism to explain the differences he observed among apparently closely-related species. Tame pigeons were a classic example of the great range of diversity being developed from a wild ancestor, the common rock dove. This diversity had been developed by human intervention, with controlled breeding. Darwin's theory proposed a natural selection process, parallel to that of human selection in the controlled breeding of tame species.

The selection process in nature resulted when individuals of a species occupying a particular environmental niche and functioning well in it, were more likely to survive and produce offspring than those not as well adapted. Eventually, the whole species had characteristics of those individuals best adapted to their environment. An interbreeding group in one environment might become quite different from a group isolated in a different environment, even though the original stock of both groups had been the same before their isolation. This is what Darwin had in mind by natural selection and the survival of the fittest. The popular mind has often distorted Darwin's ideas to mean superiority and success of the most ruthless.

Many concluded that God was not needed as Creator if Darwin's survival of the fittest was the process at work. Time and chance seemed to be in the driver's seat, with perhaps a passing nod to God at the beginning to start the whole mechanism. Darwin struggled with the ultimate meaning of his ideas, and found it very difficult to reconcile the idea of God as found in his theological studies, with the cruelty of nature, as the poet put it, "red in tooth and claw."

There have been significant developments in the knowledge of genetics since Darwin. We are now able to look at the transmission of traits from one generation to the next at the molecular level in the remarkable structure of DNA. We know about the possibility and role of mutations in changing the characteristics of living things. Still, at the base of the theory of evolution, is the role of chance, and natural selection of the traits that will survive in a population of organisms that form a species. Evolution holds that these mechanisms are the primary factors causing the development of new species.

Evolutionists maintain that the fossil record is evidence that this has occurred. Some creationists deny that new species have ever developed, and also appeal to the fossil record, saying that missing links between one species and another have never been found. These counter positions cannot be resolved without agreement as to what constitutes a species or the definition of transition forms. So-called facts by themselves do not resolve differences of philosophical presuppositions, or the elaborate webs of explanations that are woven from facts and assumptions.

Evolution is commonly accepted by most scientists, including many Christians. Still, evolution continues to be challenged by some who believe in "creation science." Creation science has been most successful in calling into question the assumption of slow, steady evolutionary change in the development of new species through transition forms. Even many evolutionists will admit that so-called "missing links" are rare in the fossil record.

The best evolutionary answer to the problem of missing links is the theory by Gould and Eldredge, called punctuated equilibrium. It maintains that during most of the time that a given species exists, its form is essentially a stable equilibrium of its genetic possibilities. In other words, they agree that most fossil organisms do not show change. However, they hold that such steady state conditions are punctuated by periods of change. If a species is essentially stable for 10 million years, and then undergoes species change in 10 thousand years, only one in a thousand of its fossils might be a transition form. This would become a rare find.[41] This view is being debated, but has gained adherents. It is little comfort to "creation scientists."

God's Order in Creation Does Not Preclude Evolution

Another argument from "creation science" has been that the third law of thermodynamics makes evolution impossible. The third law of thermodynamics holds that the universe is running down; that is, disorder, called entropy, is increasing. It explains why heat engines, like those in our motor vehicles, are always inefficient, wasting most of their energy by increasing entropy. The development of living things is a significant movement toward order, an improbable thermodynamic situation. This argument breaks down for the earth since earth is not a closed energy system, but instead soaks up energy from the sun. The energy earth absorbs from the sun makes possible a decrease of entropy on the scale of life on this planet.

Entropy and a Chess Board

Entropy is a measure of disorder or randomness in a system. This also relates to information. Consider a set of chess pieces dumped haphazardly on a chessboard. A chess player picks them up and arranges them for the beginning of a game. The entropy of the chess pieces has decreased, but in expending energy, the player has increased entropy overall, through energy losses.

Another interesting thing occurs. The arrangement of the chess pieces on the board is a kind of information, or message that can be interpreted and responded to by other players. The chance of this opening arrangement happening by dropping the pieces from a box is almost non-existent. If you don't agree, go ahead and spend the rest of your life trying to place the chess in the opening positions by dumping them haphazardly on the board.

Now let a skilled and an unskilled chess player make a few moves. Stop the action and analyze the moves. The skilled player may have set up a fool's mate (a sure win in only a few moves). Any knowledgeable player could now beat the unskilled player by completing the required moves. In fact, many novice players soon learn this play, and could beat a more skilled player if given the chance to complete the moves for the side with the sure advantage. The chess system has significant new information in relation to the original arrangement of the chess pieces.

The same results might arise from chance. Let's say that two children with no knowledge of fool's mate maneuver the pieces into this position. Since few moves are required, the probability of this occurring is quite good. The position of the pieces represents the same information, whether it is derived by chance or by human forethought. Observers seeing the positions of pieces on the board, but not having seen the play, could reach different conclusions about the cause of this condition, but no one would be likely to think that the play pieces were dropped out of a box.

Information is a somewhat subjective perception in the eyes, or at least the logic, of the beholder. If many moves were used to set up a sequence of half-a-dozen or so plays leading to a sure checkmate, only a good player would recognize the possibility of checkmate, and few would consider it a chance occurrence. This kind of thinking drives the 'intelligent design' argument, but setting seemingly impossible criteria for the role of chance is not a required criterion for making the hidden hand of God visible.

The above chess scenario is a possible model of showing the difficulty of reaching a scientific conclusion of whether chance or divine intent is the basis for living things, as we know them. Evolution maintains that natural selection of random variation explains the change of species in the fossil record, and in the diversity of life we observe. Evolution theory has not shown, and does not show, that no information came from God in this remarkable process and result.

It is interesting to note that many sections of DNA strands in a living organism are inactive genetic materials, but they may become active in later offspring. We are largely ignorant of the role of this inactive genetic material in successive forms having a common lineage in the fossil record. Though *Jurassic Park* might lead some to believe otherwise, we do not have fossil DNA, except for very recent forms. Neither science nor theology gives us a definitive account of evolution or creation at the molecular level.

We believe when we say that God created, and we believe when we say that all life evolved without the intentional oversight of God. Faith in God maintains, "In the beginning, God," but atheism says, "In the beginning, matter and energy." On the one hand, only God is eternal; on the other, one must struggle with the difficult idea that the stuff of an aging universe is eternal or somehow arose out of nothing. Doubt and belief are involved in any conclusion. There is a choice. This is at the heart of what God intends for the present. We may freely choose, and our choices will make all the difference.

The scientific study of evolution should not be considered a threat to Christian faith. At the same time, a lot that has been proposed under the name of evolution has been counter to faith because it was not really science. There is an appropriate way for science and faith to work together, but few of us find it.

Good evolutionary theory must develop and be self-correcting, like any other true science. Current biological evolutionary science has shown some of these characteristics. The study and understandings of the origins and development of living organisms appears to me to be far more complex than the study of the development of the gross structures of the universe, solar system, planets, or earth itself. Many of these sciences are but in their infancy, and certainly biological evolution still has a long way to go. Yet, evolution has made large gains since Charles Darwin's *Origin of Species* was first published in 1859.

Misleading Terminology of the Supernatural

As already discussed, I personally am a little wary of the term supernatural. The term supernatural is too often used to defend some magical cause apart from what could be scientifically or naturally explained. I do not mean by this wariness that God is contained by nature in some kind of pantheistic or animistic presence. Nature is not all there is. What occurs by God's will in nature is not somehow countermanded by God in a supernatural act. God's work apart from what we call nature is not inconsistent with God's work in nature. Nature is not some kind of wound clock that can run independent of the clockmaker. To my mind, God sustains nature, much as the life of an organism is sustained by its life-giving organic processes. Unlike the organic processes of a living organism that do not sustain themselves apart from the organism, God is self-existent quite apart from nature, which is God's creation.

The action of God in nature is always consistent with the action of God apart from nature, and vise versa. What we might want to call a supernatural act of God reveals our ignorance of God's action in nature, for there is nothing unnatural about God acting in nature. Human acts in nature are too often unnatural and contrary to what is the God-intended course of nature. Nature as an organism suffers from a disease inflicted on it by human sin that seeks to deny God's rightful place in nature. Humans can exercise a great deal of immediate causation in nature. Sometimes this is complementary to God's own causation in nature, and sometimes it is contrary to God's causation. I do not think that human beings exercise ultimate causation. This is reserved for God alone.

God does not relate to nature only in the sense of ultimate causation. This would be to limit God, which would in my estimation make God something less than God. God acts through immediate and ultimate causation in nature. God can be physically present in nature, as incarnate in Christ. Although this is the fullness of God expressed bodily, this cannot be all there is to God, who is self-existent apart from nature. What appears to us as a paradox, is evidence of our own limitation as human beings? What we want to call supernatural is also evidence of our limitations. We have not completely apprehended God at work in nature, either through immediate or ultimate causation.

God's hand appears to be hidden if we speak only of evolution. Because God's hand is required for the creation of life and the sustaining of life of all kinds, I prefer to call the natural mechanisms 'development,' implying a 'developer' rather than evolution. Development cannot be a scientific term, for science does not study this level of causation. In order to be able to speak to scientists, we may need to use the term evolution, but we see evolution only as a tool of God. Scientist and Christian scholar David Wilcox has this helpful view:

"Those who believe in God have, I maintain, fallen victim to a false dichotomy when it comes to how God operates in nature. Many feel forced to choose between 'naturalism' (materialism) and 'supernaturalism' (God). This choice has been required for many because many people have lost sight of the biblical concept that God operates in nature. I assert again that we should not have to choose between God and so-called natural causes. We can choose *both*."[42]

Indeed, when God spoke to the water to bring forth living creatures something wonderful was begun at the molecular level and replicating life came into being from 'dead' chemical reactions. God saw that it was good; so should we presume to heap scorn on the mechanism, even if it is named evolution?

God had a second phrase in the creation speech. It is, ". . .let birds fly above the earth across the dome of the sky." God also created "every winged bird of every kind." This refers not just to the kinds we know now, but also to those early birds, hundreds of millions of years ago in the Jurassic Period, that had distinctly reptilian characteristics.

God didn't specify what medium the birds were to come from, so there is no Biblical basis to deny what the fossil record clearly shows. Nor should we make a barrier out of the unscientific word "kind", or even its scientific cousin, "species." Sharp boundaries are blurred, for indeed offspring are quite recognizably like parents, but not exactly like them. This is the keyhole in creation that lets in evolution, whether we like it or not. I, for one, am quite content to sit back and hear God's blessing on the whole process.

"Be fruitful and multiply and fill the waters in the seas, and let the birds multiply on the earth." At God's expressed command

and blessing, sea creatures found new environmental niches, and exploited them well by becoming new kinds or species. Birds did a similar job of development into new kinds and species as they spread across isolated landmasses or island-hopped across the oceans. We just didn't realize how they were responding to this information from God, until Darwin observed the finches of the Galapagos, and wrote *Origin of the Species*. Maybe it is time for people of faith to give God the credit for God's own plan of creation, and not turn natural history over to atheists. "And God saw that it was good."

In Walton's view, God delegated functionaries, creatures to swim and creatures to fly, on the fifth day, but I would suggest that God also created the waters that brought forth life that became swimmers and fliers.

Let the Earth Bring Forth Animal Life (Day Six, Step 1)

Like day three, day six has two steps. Genesis 1:24-25 is the first step.

> "And God said, 'Let the earth bring forth the living creature after his kind, cattle, and creeping thing, and beast of the earth after his kind:' and it was so. And God made the beast of the earth after his kind and cattle after their kind, and every thing that creepeth upon the earth after his kind: and God saw that it was good." (KJV)

> "And God said, 'Let the earth bring forth every kind of living creature: cattle, creeping things, and wild beasts of every kind.' And it was so. God made wild beasts of every kind and cattle of every kind, and all kinds of creeping things of the earth. And God saw that it was good." (SJB)

> "And God said, 'Let the earth bring forth living creatures of every kind: cattle and creeping things and wild animals of the earth of every kind.' And it was so. God made the wild animals of the earth of every kind, and the cattle of every kind, and everything that creeps upon the ground of every kind. And God saw that it was good." (NRSV)

"And God said, 'Let the land produce living creatures according to their kinds: livestock, creatures that move along the ground, and wild animals, each according to its kind.' And it was so. God made the wild animals according to their kinds, the livestock according to their kinds, and all the creatures that move along the ground according to their kinds. And God saw that it was good." (NIV)

We are now ready to tease out God's work on the sixth day. We will begin with only the first small step, for part of this day. God's speech says, 'let the earth bring forth.' This sounds very similar to what God said about plants on the third day, and is parallel to what God said of the water on the fifth day. Land and water may appear to us as natural forms, but it seems that their Creator endowed them with the ability to be further formed into living things.

God announces cattle, creeping things, and wild animals. From geology, we know that the most primitive plants preceded animal life in the seas, which in turn preceded bird and animal life on the land. We also know that plants developed more complex forms, such as grasses and flowering plants, over billions of years, and after primitive animals. To us the more familiar cattle and wild animals are often more recent species in fossil records.

It may also be noted that in the overlap of the fifth day with the sixth day, whale and dolphin ancestors returned from land to the sea, and became very successful water dwellers, even though they are air-breathing mammals. Indeed, some of them were "great sea monsters" outstripping the largest dinosaurs in size, and are the largest creatures that ever lived on earth. I expect God enjoyed this little U-turn in creating animals; perhaps it is part of God's sense of humor. God made the birds that fly, even humming birds, as distant relatives of the terrible Tyrannosaurus Rex. Let's not reduce God's creativity to some less imaginative, human kind of engineering. The fossil record, as well as animal life, is a story that glorifies the Creator. I am not ashamed to tell it and ascribe it to the Creator.

Dinosaurs reigned for some hundred million years before our familiar mammals, but they apparently were wiped out by an asteroid collision that greatly altered their environment about 65 million years ago.[43] Lowly little mammals, which had lived in the shadows of the dinosaurs, proved more resourceful, and filled many new environmental niches with their development of many new kinds. To say only, this is evolution, is to miss the point that God intentionally made animals of every kind. We should not limit these kinds to what we see now, nor stick God with animals that always exactly replicated themselves without change over hundreds of millions of years. God's creation is dynamic, just like the results of an animal breeder, who can produce new varieties, on a shorter time scale and in fewer generations. Should we limit God to less than what humans can achieve through breeding? Nature should be seen as God's arena, and also seen as God's tools for creating animals of every kind. We should not banish God from work in nature. God, at any rate, saw that it was good.

Land — Location and Function

In Walton's view, God delegated functionaries—creatures that we call living, including cattle, creeping things and wild animals—with their own functions, on the fifth day. Though Walton suggested that land was only the location from which living creatures came, I would suggest that God also appointed land as a functionary that brought forth life made of the elements of the earth.

The functions of these living creatures are to be fecund, to reproduce themselves and fill the earth. If a pregnant animal eats a plant, it is ingesting materials absorbed from the earth, through the plant's roots. Of course the early writer was not likely thinking of this, but God who inspired the author understood all the details.

We can feel comfortable with our own richer scientific detail as we read these verses. Though the text does not imply this, science tells us that animals are from land by composition, as well as land locations. In the upcoming Bible text, God forms Adam from the dust of the earth. Is "from the dust of the earth" only a reference to place, not substance? Unlike Walton, I do relate this to the third day of creation, since the base source of all higher animal life is plant life, even for carnivores that depend on plant feeders at the bottom of their food chain.

Functionaries Installed

Creation Series, this one by Ruby Wiebe

Chapter 5

Let Us Make Human Beings in Our Image

Scripture on the creation of humans, Gen 1:26-31 (Day Six, Step 2)

"And God said; Let us make man in our image, after our likeness: and let them have dominion over the fish of the sea, and over the fowl of the air, and over the cattle, and over all the earth, and over every creeping thing that creepeth upon the earth.

So God created man in his own image, in the image of God created he him; male and female created he them.

And God blessed them, and God said unto them, Be fruitful, and multiply, and replenish the earth, and subdue it: and have dominion over the fish of the sea, and over the fowl of the air, and over every living thing that moveth upon the earth.

And God said, Behold, I have given you every herb bearing seed, which is upon the face of all the earth, and every tree, in the which is the fruit of a tree yielding seed; to you it shall be for meat.

And to every beast of the earth, and to every fowl of the air, and to every thing that creepeth upon the earth, wherein there is life, I have given every green herb for meat: and it was so.

And God saw every thing that he had made, and behold, it was very good. And the evening and the morning were the sixth day." (KJV)

"And God said, 'Let us make man in our image, after our likeness. They shall rule the fish of the sea, the birds of the sky, the cattle, the whole earth, and all the creeping things that creep on earth.'

And God created man in His image,
in the image of God He created him;
male and female He created them.

God blessed them and God said to them, 'Be fertile and increase, fill the earth and master it; and rule the fish of the sea, the birds of the sky, and all living things that creep on earth.' 29 God said, 'See, I give you every seed-bearing plant that is upon all the earth, and every tree that has seed bearing fruit; they shall be yours for food. And to all the animals on the land, to all the birds of the sky, and to everything that creeps on earth, in which there is the breath of life, [I give] all the green plant for food.' And it was so. 31 And God saw all that He had made, and found it very good. And there was evening, and there was morning, the sixth day." (SJB)

"Then God said, "Let us make humankind in our image, according to our likeness; and let them have dominion over the fish of the sea, and over the birds of the air, and over the cattle, and over all the wild animals of the earth, and over every creeping thing that creeps upon the earth."

So God created humankind in his image,
in the image of God he created them;
male and female he created them.

God blessed them, and God said to them, "Be fruitful and multiply, and fill the earth and subdue it; and have dominion over the fish of the sea and over the birds of the air and over every living thing that moves upon the earth." 29 God said, "See, I have given you every plant yielding seed that is upon the face of all the earth, and every tree with seed in its fruit; you shall have them for food. 30 And to every beast of the earth, and to every bird of the air, and to everything that creeps on the earth, everything that has the breath of life, I have given every green plant for food." And it was so. 31 God saw everything that he had made, and indeed, it was very good. And there was evening and there was morning, the sixth day." (NRSV)

"Then God said, "Let us make man in our image, in our likeness, and let them rule over the fish of the sea and the birds of the air, over the livestock, over all the earth, and over all the creatures that move along the ground."

So God created man in his own image,
in the image of God he created him;
male and female he created them.

God blessed them and said to them, "Be fruitful and increase in number; fill the earth and subdue it. Rule over the fish of the sea and the birds of the air and over every living creature that moves on the ground."

Then God said, "I give you every seed-bearing plant on the face of the whole earth and every tree that has fruit with seed in it. They will be yours for food. 30 And to all the beasts of the earth and all the birds of the air and all the creatures that move on the ground—everything that has the breath of life in it—I give every green plant for food." And it was so.

God saw all that he had made, and it was very good. And there was evening, and there was morning—the sixth day." (NIV)

Created in God's Image; Verses 26-27

God speaks an intentional word, "Let us make." This is a different wording than the words, "Let the water or the earth bring forth." In this continuation of the sixth day, we might expect a similar creature to animals to be made, but there is a very different nuance to this facet of creation.

First, there is group agreement to do something special. Who might this group be, if there is only one God? Fretheim explains this well:

"The 'let us' language refers to an image of God as a consultant of other divine beings; creation of human kind results from a dialogical act–an inner divine communication–rather than a monological one. Those who are not God are called to participate in this central act of creation. Far from either slighting divine transcendence or concealing God within the divine assembly, it reveals and enhances the richness and complexity of the divine realm. God is not in heaven alone, but is engaged in a relationship of mutuality within the divine realm, and chooses to share the creative process with others. Human beings are the product of this consultation . . . they are created in the image of one who chooses to create in a way that shares power with others"[44]

One may argue fine points of interpretation, but most commentators see their interpretations of the use of the plural as compatible with Hebrew monotheism. Christians see in this the possibility of the involvement of Christ and the Holy Spirit in creation. The singular verb for "create" does suggest that God worked alone in creation.[45] The Christian doctrine of the trinity was not intended to distract from monotheism, although some Christians may appear to make it do so.

A consultation with the heavenly court is appropriate because God is about to assign dominion over the earthly realm. God could have delegated this role to angelic beings of the heavenly court, but with their implicit agreement, God assigns dominion to a creature that the earth brought forth associated with the animals of the sixth day. This is an important point to ponder for Christian theology. It puts humans, with a clear connection with animals, in charge of the earth. Biologically, the human physical nature is clearly classified with mammals. Therefore, human beings should be compassionate to animals as God, who assumed human flesh in the Son, is compassionate to humanity.

There is another very important theological aspect of humans revealed in the words God expressed in order to make humankind in our "image and likeness." This relationship to the divine sets human beings apart from the animals, and supports their role of dominion. Its exact meaning has engendered many interpretations. These are laid out in detail by Wenham.[46] For my purposes the following provides a good summary: "The image functions to mirror God to the world, to be God as God would be to the non-human, to be an extension of God's own dominion."[47]

Note also that the word "created" is used. "*Created*, Hebrew *bara'*, a verb whose sole subject is God, here references only three objects: the universe as a whole (1.1); sea monsters, masters of the waters (1.21); and human beings, masters of land (1.27)."[48] This suggests God's being involved in an extraordinary way on these three occasions.

I also note that God made humankind masters over fish of the sea, birds of the air, and every living thing that moves on the earth. Earth in (1: 26) and (1:28) is the Hebrew, *erets,* meaning land or all the earth in contrast to heaven. So sea monsters are also mastered by humankind.

The image of God applies to both male and female. Fretheim explains that this implies that both male and female have the divine image, but that each has a special role. He even suggests that male and female images for God could be grounded in this text. [49]

There is a hidden assumption in the mind of many readers as they see the words *male* and *female*. The assumption is that God created only two first parents, one male and the other female. Though a possibility, it is not the only possibility. God may have created a population of humankind with the two sexes, male and female. Scientifically, the latter possibility is more likely. We will address this topic later.

Fill the earth, master it, rule its animals v 28

God speaks a blessing and a command to humankind. Humankind was to procreate in order to multiply, and fill the earth. Is there a categorical difference between the human beings that are born by procreation and those that were formed by God's creation? It is a false understanding of the 'natural' process of procreation that would make it categorically different from God's creation. We who were born are just as truly God's creation as the first population of humankind. Biological natural activity is part and parcel of God's own creative activity. All human beings are and were created by procreation. God gets the credit.

Fretheim notes the writer's concern regarding populating the earth. He also suggests that should the earth become filled, human responsibility would require an adjustment to new duties in the created order.[50] In the book *Creation & the Environment, author* Redekop and others suggest what some of these adjustments might be. A few of these thoughts may be found in the quotations below:

"We must ask seriously in this generation what is the population size that fills the earth, or how shall we know when we have filled the earth. A world population of two billion in 1945 is expected to grow to more than 9 billion in one lifetime.[51] "The challenge before us now is to restore the balance of human population with the rest of nature, which will help achieve the optimum life for all. . . . Limiting the number of persons on earth is the most effective means to achieve the goal of preserving (salvaging?) a sustainable, equitable, and 'high quality' natural environment."[52]

We next examine the position of human 'dominion' in creation. What we read in Genesis chapter one will later be balanced by what we read in Genesis chapter two. The picture in the present text is a strong one, often attributed to a priestly writer. Directed at Adam, it might be read as encouragement to a young person needing to assume responsibility for his environment.

The writers in Redekop's book see humans in the Genesis text as powerful priestly figures with authority equal to the ancient Eastern Kings. They are granted authority over the entire animal kingdom to subdue it and as God's agents are called to oversee and administer God's creation.[53]

Early humans adapted to their environment and had limited control over nature. Early humans did not know the authority of kings, and probably felt rather insecure in their world. Humans needed to be prepared for their role in nature in this new relationship with God.

It is only in recent generations that human control and its impact on nature has become most evident. We do have a kingly role, but it remains to be seen whether we will have the touch of king Midas, where our desired gold becomes the bane of our existence.

Perceptions related to the meaning of scripture regarding control over nature continue to shift down through the generations.

It was very good. V 29-31

God also says that green plants are given for food to humankind and every creature that has breath. Air-breathing creatures, such as us, take in oxygen to burn food for energy. Plants are the base source of that energy. Even though carnivores eat meat, their food, in the end, comes from plant eating creatures. The energy comes from the sun and is stored in the plant by the process of photosynthesis.

This passage in Genesis should not be taken as an argument that all creatures were first created as herbivores. Certainly the fossil record indicates otherwise.

Humans have the same need as animals for food for their bodies as they, too, are of the earth. Even Jesus Christ, the Son of God, needed material food, God identified with humans and also with animals. We humans should identify with God's more lowly creatures over which we have control, for we are their caretakers.

God was more than satisfied by the result of his creative work. God's hidden hand in creation produced what God saw as very good. Though we can also see evil, we should look at God's world in the same way. In fact, humans should see nature as amoral (without knowledge of good and evil), not as immoral.

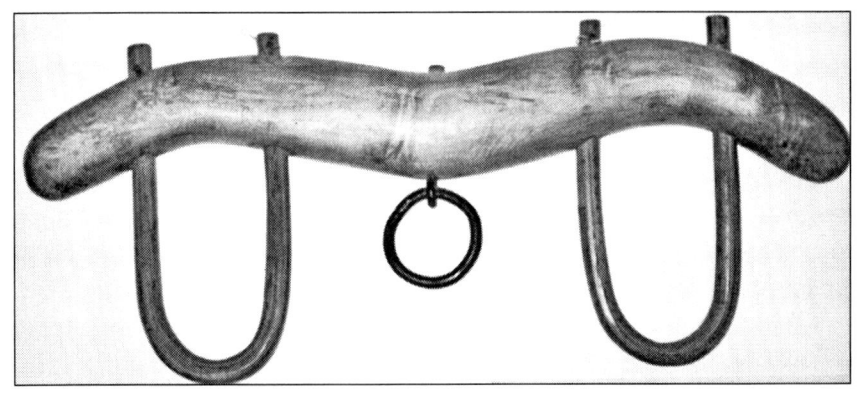

The Yoke carved by Orv Wiebe
We may yoke animals to do our will, but are earth's creatures also our yoke?

Chapter 6

God Blessed the Seventh Day as Holy

> "Thus the heavens and the earth were finished, and all their multitude. And on the seventh day God finished the work that he had done, and he rested on the seventh day from all the work that he had done. So God blessed the seventh day and hallowed it, because on it God rested from all the work that he had done in creation.
>
> These are the generations of the heavens and the earth when they were created. In the day that the LORD God made the earth and the heavens," (*NRSV*)

God blesses the day of rest Genesis 2:1-3

God's work of creating the multitudes of heaven and earth was finished. This should not be taken as a final end to the work of God. Fretheim explains this well.

"'Finishing' does not mean that God will not engage in further creative acts (the absence of the typical concluding formula cannot be appealed to, for the structure of the creation account is not exact). These days do not exhaust the divine creativity! The seventh day refers to a specific day and not to an open future. Continuing creative work will be needed, but there is a 'rounding off' of the created order at this point."[54]

God has a message in addition to the theme of creation work. It is a message of rest. Here, God's message is a clear indication that God is communicating to the experience and level of understanding of the one receiving the revelation. I doubt that many of us would think that God was tired and needed rest, but God does understand the human need for rest.

Jesus emphatically said, "The Sabbath was made for humankind, and not humankind for the Sabbath; so the Son of Man is lord even of the Sabbath." (Mark 2:27-28) Jesus was extending human dominion to the Sabbath, which corresponds well to human dominion on earth. In Genesis, the word Sabbath is not used, but the words, seventh day, are used in 2:2-3.

We need to see these verses at the beginning of chapter two as part of the same story as chapter one. Wenham confirms this below.

"In form and content the seventh day differs sharply from the preceding six. But this is no reason to make a break in the account between 1:31 and 2:1 as the medieval chapter divisions suggests. These verses make a beautifully arranged conclusion to the account of creation, echoing and balancing the opening verses. 2:1, mentioning 'heaven and earth,' and 2:3, 'which God created,' are chiastically with 1:1, and 2:2-3 with its three-fold mention of God's resting on the seventh day focus on the unique character of the day."[55]

Sabbath days were identified by their content, not necessarily by the specific count of seven days. This method of identification is again used in Leviticus 23, where religious feasts are described. The Festival of Trumpets falls on the first day of the seventh month. The Day of Atonement falls on the 10th day of the same month, and on the 15th day of the month, the Festival of Booths begins and lasts for seven days. The Day of Atonement is called a Sabbath, and other special days were given Sabbath status, even though they might not be the seventh day. It appears that the content of the day—more than the number of the day—is what constitutes a Sabbath. In addition, there are Sabbath years in Leviticus 26, showing that the length of time is not always tied to a 24-hour day.

In our Genesis text, we have the seventh day of creation as the blessed and hallowed day of rest. There is a lack of clarity in relation to the origin of the practice of the Sabbath. "Exodus 16:22-30 suggests that Israel first learned about the Sabbath in the wilderness, though Exodus 20:8, like this passage in Genesis, asserts that the Sabbath idea is as old as creation itself. In observing the seventh day as holy, man is imitating his Creator's example."[56]

Day Pattern by Content, not by Chronology and Sequence

The seven-day pattern of the Genesis text establishes a temporal order in creation, as well as a spatial order.[57] However, it is incorrect to apply a western mind-set of chronology and sequence to this order of the days. Rather, the content of the days, as is the case for the Sabbath, is what makes them different days. The situation is far more complex than the simple order of the days of the week.

Revelation and Illumination—God's Word and the Study of Science

God's revelation is of the different acts of creation, and not an account of universal or geologic history. God lets us see, as it were, a theater-in-the-round view of creation. Some scenes may overlap in time, but each is a special story of its own. The scientific story of the natural but God-directed process of creation is encyclopedic and still beyond our complete grasp. What is most significant is that God is the Creator. God has determined the functions that make heaven and earth, from subatomic particles to the heavenly bodies of the universe. God determined the energies of the universe and the relation of energy to mass. God's character that is partially revealed in this scripture, but God's hidden hand is illuminated by the study of science that shows the order and reliability of God's creative work of heaven and earth. The two, revelation and illumination, speak of what is very good about creation.

These two aspects, of God as Creator and God's hidden hand, are the drama of God's actions. They do not present a chronological description of the processes by which the physical universe came to be. The transitional verse for the two accounts, Gen. 2:4, describes creation in a "day." In the first account, creation was outlined in seven "days." Clearly, the authors and editors were not primarily concerned about time in the sense of our Western culture. Like a play, the first account moves from act to act revealing the glorious work of the creator God.

A scientific account with chronological detail would be too encyclopedic for the average person. I know of no other brief description in literature that does a better job than these accounts of Genesis in presenting the unfolding picture of the origin of the universe and earth, with all of its life.

The acts of creation outlined in the diagram below, projected on a scientific time frame, suggest something of how this drama might relate to a scientific description of origins. We have here only crudely imaginative estimates of creative activity relating the periods of the first Genesis account of creation to my oversimplified projection of a scientific chronology. Beginnings are more clearly suggested than are distinct closings of periods of creation. The curves suggest a certain increase, followed by diminution of activity for a particular dramatic episode. There is considerable overlap and interdependence of these activities.

The first act introduces light and darkness, or radiant energy and its absence. This is of great importance to the development of the structure of the universe with the function of time. The second act does not immediately follow, but shifts focus to the earth. It portrays formation of the atmosphere, with its consequences for the hydrological cycle, and the function of weather. The third act follows chronologically and consequentially with the development of continents and oceans and the rise of land plants dependent on the cycle of rain and energy of light. This provides a third major function of food.

Down through history, humans have stood in awe and even worshiped the processes that produce earth's fertility, on which we are so dependent. We speak of Mother Nature, giving her the role of a nurturing goddess. In drought, some cultures pray for rain, use incantations, follow fertility rituals, or seed the clouds. These accounts assure us that God brought about the processes of nature that gives the earth its fertility, but they do not tell us how to make rain.

The fourth act goes back to a more universal perspective, in parallel to the first act, unfolding the relationship of sun, moon, and stars to earth and humans. It portrays these objects as God's handiwork, not as a realm of gods and goddesses portrayed in human myths and fables. Scientifically, we know that stars are necessary to the formation of the elements of iron and others on the periodic chart, which are so significant to our planet and ourselves. Indeed, it has been said, that we are stardust. The formation of the sun and moon, the whole solar system in fact, some 5 to 4 billion years ago, is an act among the creation of stars so small as to have no noticeable impact on the curve for the fourth day.

The fourth act is foundational to act two and three, as well as to five and six. The fifth act shifts back to an earth perspective, and introduces living things that move through the water and air. Prior acts can be seen as an unfolding of the possibilities, in the original creation of matter and energy.

God's Creative Acts in Time
Scientific Time Line of Creation

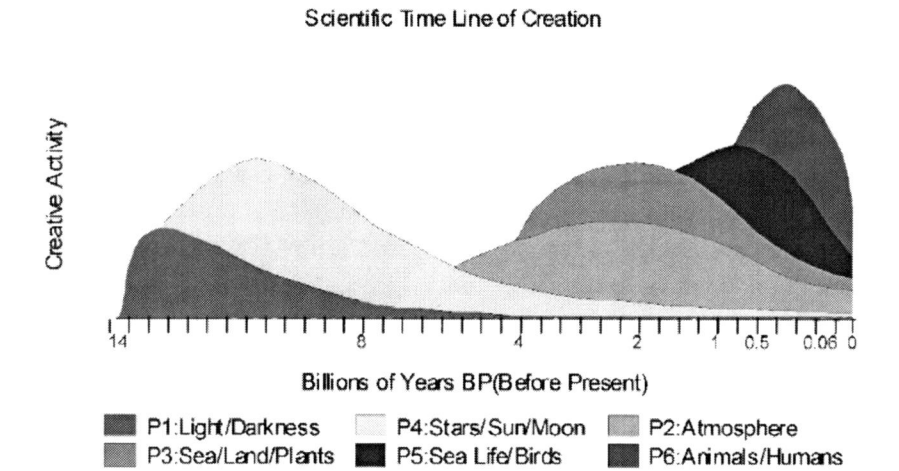

Fig. 1. A graphic portrayal of the activity of six days (periods) of Genesis spread over a logarithmic scientific time-line for the same events. The vertical axis is an inexact, imaginative presentation of creative activity. This attempts to show the complexity of the relationship of each of the six days' activity to each other. The total time is shown as approximately 14 billion years.

The living things of act five are a radical new result of creation. The sixth act follows immediately behind, with the development of all manner of animal life on the land. Through much of human history, myths have imbued animal life with characteristics of deity to be worshiped. Genesis tells us that God is the originator of all living creatures, implying that only Creator God is to be worshiped.

The sixth act has a second episode of creation. This is the creation of human beings of both sexes. They are beings, according to God's self-counsel, "in our image, our likeness." Human beings are to have responsibility for the earth and its creatures. Humans are to "subdue" the earth in the sense of mastery, as a musician who masters a musical instrument is able to bring out its full range of qualities. This command to rule over other creatures and earth, delegated to humans by the Creator, is a responsibility, not an inherent right.

Animals and humans are given the gift of plants for nourishment. Neither gender of human beings are worthy of worship, each is created, not self-existent. On our time-line, this finale of creation is so brief as to hardly show up, even though recent time is expanded on a logarithmic time scale. If the graph were expanded enough to show the drama of human creation, it would display an upward sweeping curve showing the population explosion.

The seventh act is not shown. It is outside the purview of science. It is a great celebration of all that has been accomplished. The ultimate result of day seven is the incarnation of Christ, which is not completely known in the Bible until the New Testament. God comes to be physically present with us as Jesus, the Jewish Messiah, and to Greek, the Christ. It is a hallowed time. Though the curtain is drawn at this point in the drama, it is not ended. Time unfolds before us, moving us well beyond the realm of science into that of theology.

If we follow Walton, God's creating is not the doing of physical acts of creation, but is setting up and assigning functions. This could be in 24-hour days, but God's days are not tied to our conception of time. Walton maintains that people of ancient cultures would have had an immediate understanding of what appears to us to be a shift to a very different kind of day, on the seventh day of creation.

Compare this again with the story of Joseph who, after being given the function of power over Egypt's food supply, did not return to prison, but like his former fellow prisoner was set up in royal accommodations. In our experience, this would be like being inaugurated as a new president, and moving into the White House. Ancient cultures expected their gods to spend six days in functional preparation, and then move into the temple to be worshiped.

The seventh day is the place of divine rest, but also of ongoing divine work. The temple becomes a microcosm or image of and connection to the cosmos. It relates to the functions of the cosmos. The building of temples in ancient cultures corresponds to God's creation and ordering of the cosmos, the way the White House relates to the United States.

The Generations of the Heavens and the Earth (Genesis 2:4a)

Wenham sees the opening clause 'This is the history [generations] of X' in Genesis as a heading to a cycle of narratives or a genealogy. However, both ancient and modern commentators regard it as a postscript to what precedes it—the account of creation in Genesis 1:1-2:3. They argue that 2:4a makes a neat *inclusio* with 1:1. Wenham is of the opinion that the opening clause fulfills the customary function of a heading to what follows."[58]

Fretheim construes the whole of v 4 as a hinge, looking both backward and forward.[59] This may be a good compromise position, but I favor the NRSV division between v 4a and v 4b, functioning as a pericope. In any case, this narrative movement leads to a very different account, one that is usually considered a second creation account. How we see this separation will affect how we view the second narrative.

How the two accounts relate to each other becomes the significant question. Is day six expanded in the new account, but really the same day? Or might the new account be wholly its own account, but much later than the creation activities of the sixth day? Is the male of humankind found in day six the same as Adam in the new account? For some this is a crucial theological question. If 2:4a sums up creation and completes it, then, perhaps, 2:4b opens an account in a new setting and time. In this case Adam may not be the first human. We will explore this issue in the next chapter.

Chapter 7

God, Adam & Eve in Relationship

Gen. 2:4b-14 begins a new story.

"In the day that the Lord God made the earth and the heavens, 5 when no plant of the field was yet in the earth and no herb of the field had yet sprung up—for the Lord God had not caused it to rain upon the earth, and there was no one to till the ground; 6 but a stream would rise from the earth, and water the whole face of the ground—7 then the Lord God formed man from the dust of the ground, and breathed into his nostrils the breath of life; and the man became a living being. 8 And the Lord God planted a garden in Eden, in the east; and there he put the man whom he had formed. 9 Out of the ground the Lord God made to grow every tree that is pleasant to the sight and good for food, the tree of life also in the midst of the garden, and the tree of the knowledge of good and evil.

10 A river flows out of Eden to water the garden, and from there it divides and becomes four branches. 11 The name of the first is Pishon; it is the one that flows around the whole land of Havilah, where there is gold; 12 and the gold of that land is good; bdellium and onyx stone are there. 13 The name of the second river is Gihon; it is the one that flows around the whole land of Cush. 14 The name of the third river is Tigris, which flows east of Assyria. And the fourth river is the Euphrates." (NRSV)

No One to Till the Ground (Gen. 2:4b-6)

According to Fretheim, verse 2:4b identifies God in a new way. His observation about the names used for God makes a significant point.

Elohim, the generic term for the deity, occurs throughout 1:1-2:3. In linking the names Yahweh and Elohim [LORD God] in 2:4-25, the writer may have intended to identify Israel's special name for God with the creator of the world (allowing Elohim to stand alone in 1:1-2:3 makes it clear that we are dealing with pre-Israel realities).[60] This shows a movement from a universal story of creation, where the name for God, Hebrew *Elohim*, is used by itself, to a story of a particular family that begins with Adam and Eve; where Israel's special name for God is linked with the universal Creator of the world *Yahweh Elohim*. There also is a shift in word order from "heaven and earth" to "earth and heaven." There are differences in literary type, structure, style, and vocabulary. The center of concern is different. There are also key similarities.[61] All of these are important in determining the relationship between the two stories.

The Bountiful Garden
Engraving by Dutch Mennonite artist Jan Lukyn (1649-1712)

A simple word count (see Table 1 below) of the subjects and verbs related to the activity of the first account help paint a picture of what the account is really about. It clearly is about God, Hebrew

(Elohim). God is the primary character, and responsible for all that is done. God is the one acting. Any other actions are simply responses following God's commands, such as the earth bringing forth vegetation, in v. 12. The nouns and verbs for such responsive action are not counted.

Although we often call verse 2:4b a creation account, the verbs tell of different kinds of actions. The verbs of what God said and saw are found most frequently. Created comes in third, tying with the verb made, or make.

TABLE 1
NOUNS, PRONOUNS AND VERBS
USED IN GENESIS 1:1-2:4a

NOUN/PRONOUN	WORD COUNT	VERB	WORD COUNT
God *Elohim*	35	said	10
He	3	saw	7
God implied	1	created *bara'*	6
Us	_1_	made/make *'asâ*	5
	40	called	4
		blessed	3
		rested	2
		separated	2(+3)
		finished	2
		set	1
		swept	_1_
			43

Kidner writes that the word for created, Hebrew *bārā'*, in the Old Testament invariably has God as the subject, and the results can be things or situations. This impressive verb marks three significant beginnings in the first account, but does not show a particular way of creating, since it is parallel with the verb make, Hebrew *'āśâ*, in 2:3-4 that covers the whole range of God's work.[62] God's actions of (created, made/make) are only about one quarter of what God is doing in the text. The account is clearly telling that the aspects of the heavens and the earth being described are from God, whether created or said or something else.

TABLE 2
NOUNS, PRONOUNS AND VERBS
USED IN GENESIS 2:4b-25

NOUN/PRONOUN	WORD COUNT	VERB	WORD COUNT
LORD God *Yahweh Elohim*	11	took	4
God implied	5	formed	3
He	4	made/make *'asâ*	2
I	_1_	brought	2
	21	caused	2
		put	2
		made to grow	1
		made/build	1
		breathed	1
		closed	1
		commanded	1
		planted	1
		said	1
		see	_1_
			23

The word pictures of this first creation story focus on God the actor, rather than on the result of the action we call creation. Perhaps it should be called the Creator account. Creation is mentioned to tell us about God, not about the world. It is not intended to be a scientific textbook about the nature of the world.

A word count (see Table 2 above) of the subject and verbs related to the activity of the second account help us see what this account is really about. The primary character is identified as the LORD God, Hebrew *Yahweh Elohim*. There is some minor action besides what God does, such as the man naming the animals, but these words are not counted in the table. The account never uses the Hebrew word created, *bara*, but uses made, or make, or formed, a number of times. Most of the other actions relate to things that already exist. It would be a misnomer to call this a creation account. The actions in the second account are often very different and distinct from the actions of the first account. God is identified by a different Hebrew name in the second account. We need to look more closely at the story line to understand the primary focus of the second account.

Even admitting that there are some similarities to the two stories, the differences are even greater, and they suggest a new story in a new time and a new place. The dry condition of the earth, man being formed before plants and animals are formed, animals coming next to last, and woman last of all is a very different sequence of events, if taken literally, from the first account. Those who seek to make this the same story as the sixth day of creation, have to take one or the other account in a non-literal way. Many do not take the time sequence of the account of chapter two as literal. It does seem odd to take other aspects of the story, such as the formation of the woman from the rib of the man, in a literal way. Doing so suggests that we bring pre-conceived interpretations to our reading.

I conclude that "the day that the LORD God made the earth and the heavens" is an indefinite extended time, and that the new account now focuses on earth or land to expand its story to this new time and place. This place was not at first hospitable to human life, there were no plants, no life-giving rain, and no one to take care of or till the ground or soil. At times, this otherwise barren place was flooded, by rising stream waters. The text may not be saying that the whole earth was such a wasteland, but only that this part of the earth or land was not vegetated and productive.

Archeological Dating of the Genesis Story

There is one archeological clue as to the time when these events may have happened. It is in the word 'till,' which suggests knowledge of agriculture. The earliest humans were hunters and gatherers, while more settled living, with soil preparation and planting crops, came later.

In the "Holy Land," which we will take as typical of the broader region: archeology suggests some early dates for the beginning of cultivation of crops. Archeology gives a rough time frame for the development of agriculture and tilling the land, as explained by Thomas Levy, editor, in *The Archaeology of Society in the Holy Land*.

"Establishing Neolithic sedentary communities in the Jordan Valley, the first farmers gained the use of flat river lands as fields. The main considerations in choosing a location were primarily related to cereal cultivation. The growth of agricultural villages and the development of new communities are archaeologically visible during the ninth millennium BP, (Before Present) but become clearer by the end of the eighth millennium BP."[63]

The date for sedentary agriculture relates to when tilling the soil became common. This may set something of an outside limit for the earliest dating of the Garden of Eden to eight or nine thousand years ago, if we assume that the idea of tilling comes from the original story and not from the writing of a later author such as Moses, or a redactor from a much later period of Israel's history. In a later chapter of Genesis, the mention of bronze and iron tools, several generations after Adam, correspondingly sets an inside date limit. The use of bronze dates to the Chalcolithic period or "sometime between 4,500—4,000 BCE . . ."[64] Thus, it appears reasonable to set the garden story around 5,000 to 8,000 years ago.

Early agricultural settlements on the alluvial plain of a river provided the kind of watering of a stream rising and watering the ground noted in v 6. In a rough way, we now have a location and timeframe for the story that we are studying. In a gentle flooding, soil is enriched by new silt and watered. This provides for a natural renewing such as has been common in Egypt for millennia, forming a basis for rich agriculture.

After a large flood, new soil washed up from a stream may have covered the plain surrounding the river more widely, with coarser and denser materials. Large floods often result in years of a higher, dryer wasteland with few plants. The Genesis description of land before the formation of the man seems to indicate such large flooding in the setting of a river valley.

The Lord God Formed Man/Adam from the Dust of the Ground (Gen. 2:7)

"Unlike the majestic sovereign of Genesis 1, here the Lord God (Yahweh Elohim) is pictured as a potter who *forms* the man/Adam out of the ground and blows into him the breath of life." [65] Job complains to God in Job 10:9: "Remember that you fashioned me like clay; and will turn me to dust again." God is in an intimate relationship with man, and man in return is in an intimate relationship with the ground.

Clay images of human beings and of animals are found at the sites of early pottery makers in agricultural communities.[66] A skilled artisan, such as a potter, produces a form or external shape or image. Images were popular in many later cultures, and often are thought to be objects of worship. In the Pentateuch, warnings against idol worship and the making of images are common. Apparently the temptation to make and worship images was common. We may find this strange, but we likely do not attribute magical powers to images in the same way that early cultures did, even though our culture is saturated with images of media. The commonness of images in modern life may have a role in our present attitudes towards them. When images represented uncommon workmanship, they may have carried more significance, particularly in a spiritual way.

The form of an image presumably communicated something about the god that it represented. In addition, they often represented something about the human beings who made them. In creation, the form of Adam represented something about the image of God, who formed Adam.

According to Professor James Engle, the formation of *'adam* from *'adamah* in Genesis 2 is a literary device comparable to saying earthling from earth. Ron Guengerich, an Old Testament teacher and pastor, describes this in more detail.

"A pun in Hebrew that emphasizes the relationship of the human to the earth is *'adam* (human) is created out of the *'adamah* (humus). This human is an 'earth creature,' with God activating breath. The word *'adam* (from which we get the name *Adam*) has been translated as *man*. It means *man* in the sense of *human, humanity, humankind*, and not *man-as-male*. The word for male does not occur [in this chapter] until *'adam* (the human) makes the distinction between woman and man in 2:23."[67]

The formation of man/Adam from dust is a word picture like that of a potter forming a clay pot. Dust of the ground, or wet clay, while having the elements found in a human body would never have the correct compositional proportion of these elements of a human body or its complex molecular and physical structure. There is no magic transformation instantly transforming dust or earth into a human being. The nine-month process of actual formation of a human from the elements of earth is a wonderful enough event for me to call it a creation.

Creation is involved when a mother eats food, plants grow in the earth and air, and animals grow by eating plants. The plants derive their chemicals from the soil and from the wonders of photosynthesis, dependent on the composition of the earth and energy from the sun. A woman's digestive system breaks food into basic units, which are absorbed into her blood and carried to the developing embryo through a marvelously selective placenta. The new being's unique genetic instructions now give rise to living body tissue, going through many generations of cell divisions and stages of embryonic development, until a full-term baby is born. An attendant to the birthing process takes the new little chap, and may smack its bottom so that it sucks in its first breath of air and lets out a cry, announcing that it is a living being.

Something like that happened for Adam, though not in a modern delivery room. For a biochemist interested in composition, not just appearance, the creation story is a tiny hint of encyclopedic chemical complexity. The scripture does not tell us details of chemistry, but says that human beings belong to the earth, even though we are living, breathing creatures. Some think that "breathed into by God" hints at the spiritual nature of humans, or differentiates us from animals.

Difference between Human Beings and Animals

Wenham explains what distinguishes human beings from animals.

"It is not man's possession of 'the breath of life' or his status as a living 'creature' that differentiates him from the animals (*pace* T. C. Mitchell, VT 11 [1961] 186). Animals are described in exactly the same terms. Gen 1:26—28 affirms the uniqueness of man by stating that man alone is made in God's image and by giving man authority over the animals. There may be a similar suggestion here, in that man alone receives the breath of God directly (cf. 2:7 and 2:19). Man's authority over the animals is evident in that he is authorized to name them.[68]

The "special creation" view of this account that of humans created by a totally different process than animals purports to establish a chasm between humans and animals. It views humans as so distinct that they have little connection with animals, with even only a superficial relation to mammals. Such a view makes it especially abhorrent to link humans and the great apes. Being likened to a monkey is the height of indignity, a put-down. The "special creation" view also places humans come to life through human birth as somehow inferior to Adam and Eve, who were specially created.

Compare the Genesis text to the thought in Psalm 139:15-16. The Psalmist speaks of being formed in the depths of the earth, though he earlier says that he was knit together in his mother's womb. Both accounts reach for a more fundamental process than growth in a mother's womb. Genesis 2 ignores the process of development in the womb. Both suggest a fundamental relation to the earth, and its substance.

Science pushes this even further in that many of the elements essential to our bodies were formed in stars before they became part of the earth. The human body is more wonderfully made than those who gave us this account or the Psalmist could ever know.

The author is reaching for something beyond the wonder of the human body, a glimmer of what makes this human person distinct from the animals. The author may be trying to understand more fully what being in the image of God means. The author paints an inspired picture of God breathing life into man. God has entered into a relationship with this lump of humus. God is a source of life that is greater than the possibilities of Adam's physical composition in common with the animals of the garden. In this relationship with God, the Creator, there is the possibility of life beyond all that the author knows or understands.

Even evolutionary scientists agree that humans have characteristics that set them apart from animals. *Homo sapiens* have a brain that is considered unique in the animal kingdom. Science has established various methods of measurement to make this point. Brain size is not an adequate method of measure, since elephants and whales have a larger endowment than human beings. However, using a scale developed to indicate normal brain size to body-weight, we rise far above the norm.[69]

Taking into consideration the parts of the brain most involved in reason, humans are superior to other animals. This only highlights the obvious; most of us suffer no inferiority complex to animals. The gap between humans and animals in our social, cultural, and scientific development is beyond question.[70] So why belabor, or even fear something so obvious?

It is really not shocking that we are part of the animal kingdom classified as mammals. Biologically, we are correctly considered a branch from the same stock as the great apes, whether the model is evolutionary, or simply taxonomic. Even the correlation between mice and humans is so great that mice habitually suffer as stand-ins for us in many biological and psychological experiments.

The fossil record of changing life is not a value scale, with superior creatures developing most recently and inferior ones at its beginnings. It does show some more complex forms in its later stages, including humans, recognized to be the Johnny-come-lately.

Development of the automobile is something of a crude model of changing life. Can you picture a Ford Taurus becoming embarrassed on finding a Model-T Ford in its lineage, or a Cadillac denying that it shares any part of its family tree with a Chevrolet? Just ask a car collector to trade you a Tucker for a Saturn!

My point is that classification and lineage do not give us a safe place to draw up battle lines in defense of human value. The Genesis text focuses the value question in relation to the Creator, not in separation from the rest of creation. It is time to put to rest the monkey, man controversy!

It would be impossible to identify Adam and Eve in the fossil record, even if some paleontologist were to stumble across their bones. There is no scientific reason to think that Adam and Eve were different from other *Homo sapiens*. If you and I were not created because we came into the world through the normal biological process of conception, gestation, and birth, then Adam and Eve would not be created if they had a normal biological process of development. I would not want to propose the kind of theology that says that God functioned as the midwife for Adam, but somehow failed to show up when I appeared, leaving Mother Nature to do all of the work!

There are natural processes that for the intents and purposes of science appear to go along quite smoothly, without a miraculous intervention of God. As a passenger in an airplane, I really don't know whether it is flying on autopilot, or is being flown by a human pilot. My concern is that I get to my destination safely. Even if I never see the pilot or the flight controller in the control tower, I put my very life into their hands. In a similar way I trust God as my Creator, as well as the Creator of Adam and Eve.

Soul Separated From Body?

What about the concept of the human soul? Kidner explains this well.

"Man neither 'has' a soul nor 'has' a body, although for convenience he may be analyzed into two or more constituents (*e.g.* I Thessalonians 5:23). The truth here: he is a unity. *Nepeš*, translated *being* (RSV) or *soul* (AV, RV), is often the equivalent of 'life', and often of 'person' or 'self', the creature who is alive."[71]

Language of Gender

The Hebrew `ādām, or man, as used in the context of Genesis 2:7, cannot be clearly shown to mean only the male. This Hebrew word is generally used to designate human, which suggests the possibility that this portion of the story could apply to both sexes. Later, in 2:23, the Hebrew word *ish* clearly applies to man-as-male, in contradistinction to woman. The Hebrew `ādām is also used in 3:22 when the Lord God said ". . .the man has become like one of us," and clearly appears to apply to both the man and the woman. In v 24, we would not conclude that only the man, Adam, was driven out of the garden, leaving the woman, Eve, behind in the garden. It is therefore not far-fetched to say that both man and woman were formed from the ground, and later placed in the Garden of Eden, nor that this formation of humans was through the natural human birth process. At a later point, we will further consider the separate account of woman being formed from man.

Adam and Eve Not the First Human Beings

My approach may raise all sorts of theological questions: since I am implying that Adam was a real person, but not the first human, and that we may not all be his descendants. The Genesis account is simple, and gives no pretense to speculation about the profound meanings that may be involved. It is direct, and leaves unanswered a multitude of questions we may ask. Most adults cannot read this simple story without supplying answers grown out of childish speculation or inherited traditions of explanation.

You may be shocked at my suggestion that Adam had parents. You may have "always" thought that Adam was the first man. Why? Many readers of the creation account in chapter 1 and the account in chapter 2 have merged the two aspects of the same set of "beginnings." Simple observation requires a first man and first women, followed by the natural cycle of birth and death from generation to generation.

My point is that we have difficulty looking at the story without overlaying many presuppositions. It is helpful to peel away that which does not come directly from the story. Our presuppositions create most of the "problems" in reconciling this primitive account with a more scientific view. Admittedly, I am consciously substituting scientific presuppositions when I accept a scientific account of origins. The original story, taken as a primitive, pre-scientific account, fully human and fully inspired, is compatible with what is known about human origins based on scientific evidence. One need not think of Adam as the first biological human being. The text of the story does not say he was the first man. It does say or imply that God created man. It does not spell out the steps in his creation in scientific language, although it indicates that man's substance is that of common, earthly materials. I find the following by Kidner helpful:

. . .the unity of mankind 'in Adam' and our common status as sinners through his offence are expressed in Scripture in terms not of heredity but simply of solidarity. We nowhere find applied to us any argument from physical descent such as that of Hebrews 7:9, 10 (where Levi shares in Abraham's act through being 'still in the loins of his ancestor'). Rather, Adam's sin is shown to have implicated all men because he was the federal head of humanity, somewhat as in Christ's death 'one died for all, therefore all died' (2Cor. 5:14). Paternity plays no part in making Adam 'the figure of him that was to come' (Rom. 5:14).[72]

Theologically this is a reasonable position. Scientifically, I do not intend an extensive discussion of human origins, but do let us consider some basic information.

Scientific Evidence of The Origins of Humankind

There is abundant scientific evidence of humans, identified as the species *Homo sapiens*, having lived long before the 6,000 years ago at which most, rather literal, interpretations of Genesis would place Adam. The study of genes and fossils tells us that Africa was our birthplace some 200,000 years ago. Some humans left Africa a good 50,000–70,000 years ago. These migrants followed a southern Asia coastal route, and reached Australia nearly 50,000 years ago. Others pushed into Central Asia, to the steppes north of the Himalaya, around 40,000 years ago. Asian immigrants seeded

Europe 30,000–40,000 years ago. Finally, the Americas were populated 15,000–20,000 years ago.[73]

Earlier pre-modern humans, the Neandertals (older spelling Neanderthals), also came out of Africa. In Europe, the two races or species overlapped, but eventually the Neandertals lost out. "On current evidence, the two groups interbred rarely, if at all. Neither mitochondrial DNA from Neandertal fossils nor modern human DNA bears any trace of an ancient mingling of bloodlines."[74] There is significant evidence that groups of modern humans roamed the southern Levant 10,000–20,000 years ago.[75] "Sites in Israel hold the earliest evidence of modern humans outside of Africa, but that group went no farther, dying out about 90,000 years ago."[76]

Abraham was the ancient ancestor of the Jewish people. He wandered around the Fertile Crescent, from the city of Ur in southern Mesopotamia, then northward through Assyria, westward through Syria, southward into Palestine and into Egypt to escape famine, but then returned to Palestine. His ancestors in Mesopotamia lived there about 6,000 years ago due to conditions essential for civilization: water and arable land.[77]

It is Abraham's ancestors, not the earliest human beings that we can connect to the usual Biblical time of Adam. The Hebrew Bible relates the account of human origins to the culture and people from whom we have received the Hebrew Bible as part of the Christian Bible. It appears to me that the Genesis 2 account relates biologically to this Jewish family tree, but does not necessarily relate to the biological origins of all people. However, the meaning and theology of Genesis are for all cultures and all peoples.

The LORD God Planted a Garden in Eden (Gen. 2:8)

The Genesis story continues to identify a place called Eden, where God planted a garden. The wasteland that was without plants became the garden of God. The garden is likely a special area within Eden and not the whole of Eden. "...the establishment of the garden for man more closely parallels the provision of food for him in 1:29 than the creation of plants in 1:12-13. . . . The use of the preposition 'in' shows Eden is understood as the name of the area in which the garden was planted."[78] The phrase 'in Eden' may simply mean a wider 'luxuriant', geographical area, although 3:22-24 seems to equate Eden with the garden.[79]

As a boy I explored and played in a neglected, rocky pasture on the hillside opposite my home. Many years later my wife, Susan, and I built our dream home on that very hillside which was now wooded. Over the years, God planted many kinds of trees on this weedy wasteland. Squirrels carried in walnuts and acorns. Birds dropped cedar and other seeds their systems could not digest. The wind blew in maple and other winged seeds. We found seedlings of cultivated plants located on the Eastern side of the hill the Park View suburb of Harrisonburg and EMU campus are located on. Under the shade of these growing trees, wildflowers bloomed, and mosses found enough moisture to thrive. There was even a flowering pear tree. God gave us a little Garden of Eden on that hillside planted by God's own natural agents and un-named Johnny Appleseeds.

Genesis also reports the location of the Garden of Eden to be 'in the east.' This might have been east of Israel, in Arabia or Mesopotamia. Assuming for a moment the author of Genesis to be Moses, he is recording this for a group of persons who have lived for centuries in Egypt, so the east could even have been the flood plain of the Jordan. If an early oral reporter reported the location, the east might be in still a different location. Moreover, the whole of Eden as a luxuriant area might be the whole Fertile Crescent, from Egypt to Mesopotamia, with the garden in its eastern portion.

It is in this luxuriant, green carpet setting that God places this particular man and woman God had formed. This man and woman will have a distinct role and place in the history of the human race, as we have the story from the biblical perspective. Although God spoke a blessing and command to the human beings of chapter one, it is not specifically recorded which, if any, of these persons heard or understood what God said.

Further on in the second account, we get a clear report of an interaction between a human and God. It is the first reported meeting of a human being with his or her Maker. It was to be an important meeting for God, and God prepared for this welcome to Adam by rolling out the green carpet. The rest of Genesis and the Pentateuch, as well as later accounts of the Hebrew Bible, report God's meetings with selected human beings. Why should we imagine that there were no other human beings than those selected by God for some special purpose of God's own choosing? Selection by God to face the ethical choice of the garden gives Adam and Eve a special place in the story of salvation. It is this choice of God, rather than Adam and Eve being the first biological humans that makes this story important for all humans. It is also why this story is placed so early in the Biblical account.

Every Tree and the Trees of Life and of Knowledge (Genesis 2:9)

God chose special trees for this wonderful garden, prepared as an ideal environment for the human of humus, the earthling from earth. There were trees chosen for their beautiful appearance, and trees chosen as particularly good for food. Certainly when God planted the garden, there were many other plants we would not call trees. God paid attention to them, and caused them to grow. The garden had to have appropriate nutrients, sunlight and water to grow well. Healthy plants made for healthy humans. Attractive plants contributed to an aesthetically pleasing environment that aided a healthy human spirit. This is not the formalized thinking of the first story but a more free, imaginative and intuitive account.

Two unusual trees are introduced: the tree of life in the midst of the garden and the tree of the knowledge of good and evil. Surely this means more than botanical trees, but rather symbolic trees: one tree representing life and the other, moral discernment of good from evil. The storyteller is preparing us for a dramatic turn of events that will relate to these two trees. We are left hanging for a while as the rest of the story unfolds. We will be distracted by rivers, spice and jewels, animals, a lonely man, a woman, and marriage before the storyteller comes back to these significant trees, except to say that the fruit of one is prohibited.

Rivers of Eden (Gen. 2:10-14)

The storyteller has a well-developed sense of place. The river in the garden is important to her. She knows the source-rivers, but we find several of them to be obscure, and impossible to identify today. The Tigris and Euphrates are known, and make sense as the setting of the cradle of Mesopotamian civilization. Perhaps the river system was greatly altered by geologic events associated with Noah's flood. The original storyteller would have no knowledge of these changes. Later tellers of the story, like Moses, could only repeat the story as accurately as possible, regardless of whether it made sense with their known geography.

The storyteller is also attracted to, or at least notices, the valuable products coming from the region of the first river she names. This is in harmony with her appreciation of pleasing trees, and those providing good food noted in the section above. The storyteller has a finely developed aesthetic sense.

The identification of Cush is not clear. In the genealogy of Genesis 10, Cush is the name of a son of Ham, and the father of Havilah. Another Cush, likely a different person, is said to be the father of Nimrod. These names would come from a time many years after the earliest teller of the story. Persons retelling the story to later generations would likely have changed geographic designations to correspond to those familiar to their listeners. Some persons identify Cush with Kish of the lower Mesopotamian region, but in many places in the Bible, it means the area of Ethiopia. Havilah, with its gold, may be the Arabian Peninsula, but some think it was in Persia.

The storyteller would likely have known the area by the names of persons who settled the area in her lifetime. She may have followed with keen interest the exploration and settlements of her own descendants. An oral story is less rigidly fixed than a written story. Geographic names can be expected to have evolved in tune with the common speech of the times. The names we have in the Genesis account may well be those of the time the oral tradition was first written. This may date to the time of Moses; perhaps earlier or later.

Asshur is well known as an ancient capital city of Assyria south of Nineveh, along the Tigris River. The Euphrates is the mother river to this cradle of civilization. Some scholars locate Eden in an area just north of the Persian Gulf.

Another possibility exists for the location of Eden. Science locates the origin of our species in Africa. If this account is older than even the beginnings of the civilizations of Mesopotamia, we might see how it could be in an African setting. Some scholars have identified the Gihon River as the Nile. As mentioned above, Cush often means Ethiopia. The Blue Nile originates in Ethiopia. Perhaps the rivers associated with Eden were tributaries of the Nile. This may be the cradle of *Homo sapiens* in Africa.

The garden was guarded on the eastern side after the expulsion, indicating it would likely have been approached by a people coming from further to the east. Cain is said to have settled east of Eden. This suggests a migration eastward, which eventually would have pushed north and east through the Fertile Crescent. Primitive sites of early cultures are dotted across ancient Palestine eastward to Mesopotamia. Immigrants tend to take the names from their homelands, and apply them to their new territories. So an older Tigris (Hiddekel), and Euphrates may be preserved in the territory of Mesopotamia, because it reminded outcasts of Eden of the original home of their ancestors.

What the storyteller would have recognized as names from her home area may have been imposed on the home of later descendants. But to her and all who followed, that home's very heart, the paradise of Eden, was lost. The fact that details are mentioned related to rivers and geographic names, is itself a testimony to a human longing for a lost world that can never be recovered. This account about Adam in Eden is from its early telling tainted with that sense of a place beyond the storyteller's reach. The rivers should lead us to the very spot of the garden, but instead they distract and befuddle us geographically. Kidner gives us a glimpse of the cultural background beyond Eden:

"Greater cultural development is intended for man when the narrative momentarily (10-14) breaks out of Eden to open up a vista into a diversity of countries and resources. This discloses that there is more than primitive simplicity in store for the race: a complexity of unequally distributed skills and peoples, even if the reader knows the irony of it in the tragic connotations of the words 'gold', 'Assyria', 'Euphrates.'[80]

This storyteller knows life outside Eden. ". . .the worlds out beyond Eden already have names, suggesting that they were believed to be inhabited . . .Rivers and places no longer known to us [Pishon, Gihon, Havilah, and Cush] combine with the known – Assyria and the Tigris-Euphrates valley."[81] ". . .the final editor of Genesis 2 thought of Eden also as a real place, even if it is beyond the wit of modern writers to locate."[82]

It may be misplaced effort to attempt to further locate the garden. We can't go back, but frankly, I wouldn't want to go back to live there, even though I accept it as being a real place somewhere in Africa, or more likely the Fertile Crescent of the biblical world.

The garden story was inspired by God, to a specific people, with a specific culture. It has meaning for all people, but may not represent the actual history of us all. Christians accept a Jewish Jesus as important for us all. We may never know the whole creation story historically, but it is important for us all.

Man Put in the Garden to Till It and Keep It (Gen.2:15)

Note that God took a particular human, and placed him in the garden. He was not created in the garden. He may well have had a life history of some years before he was placed in the garden. Part of this history may have been childhood development in association with a mother and a father. This simply is not important to the account. The storyteller has already made clear the ultimate human origin from humus, i.e., the common organic materials from the earth. She has noted the even more important aspect of that origin in the deliberate action of God. Now it is again God's act that makes this particular human into a consciously responsible person with a name, Adam.

Using Adam as a name emphasizes the personal relationship between God and the man. It would be a very impersonal relationship if God would not use a name, but only refer to him as the man or the human. If God was giving Adam an assigned task in the garden, the story seems to be moving to a more personal level. However, there is no grammatical structure to suggest this change in Genesis 2:4 as shown below by Fretheim.

"The point at which `ādām becomes the proper name Adam remains uncertain. Genesis 4:25 provides the first unequivocal instance of `ādām without the definite article (so NRSV), though the NRSV footnotes for 2:20 (NIV begins Adam here); 3:17 (so RSV); and 3:21 (so NEB). These three texts are ambiguous (the NIV also uses the proper name in 3:20 and 4:1, but footnotes "the man"). The movement of the meaning of `ādām back and forth between generic humankind (1:26-27; 5:1-2), the first man, and Adam probably reflects an effort both to tell a story of the past and to provide a mirroring story for every age."[83]

Adam was to work in the garden, and to take care of it. The garden was for him, but he also was for the garden. Adam was no longer just a human child; he was to become a responsible adult. He was made aware of the privileges and obligations that were his in the garden.

The story unfolds in a special setting, a garden planted by God. God placed the hero, Adam, in this garden in the east, in Eden. Adam is the one with whom God related in a personal way. In our terms, Adam has been socialized by God. This socialization is to be formed, in the best sense of the word. Human beings are not pre-programmed with many instincts, but develop in relationship with other persons. It was necessary for God to enter into such a socializing relationship with Adam in order for Adam to assume a place of accountability and responsibility in creation. There was no magic in God's words in creating human beings that made them responsible for creation. It is God's personal relationship that results in Adam's awareness of responsibility. The responsibility of work is a blessing.

Wenham notes that humans were to work before the fall. Some myths considered work a task to relieve the gods. But Genesis gives no hint that God is shifting a workload onto people. "Work is intrinsic to human life."[84]

The human must take up responsible work in God's creation. This requires good communication with the One to whom he is responsible. The work has meaning because it is participation with God in the continuation of Creation. ". . . this role involves not simple maintenance or preservation, but a part of the creative process itself. The role given the human in v 15 may be compared to the dominion/servant role in 1:28."[85] This human, Adam, and all humans are called to be actors, not just spectators, in the "eighth day" of creation. This theme is developed in the second Genesis account. This moves us well beyond the realm of science into that of theology, to be discussed in a coming section.

You May Freely Eat but Not of One Tree (Gen. 2:16-17)

There are limits to freedom that result in responsibility and accountability. The comments by Fretheim below, suggest that this relates to the place and role of creatures in the garden.

God addresses the man in vv. 16-17, giving him permission to eat from every tree except the tree of knowledge. The prohibition constitutes a version of the first commandment, a concern not evident in chapter 1. God's does not center on God's place in the world, but focuses instead on the creatures, on their place and role, and the gifts they are given. God expresses no concern that the creature might exalt itself at God's expense.[86]

Those human beings that preceded Adam could not be held responsible or accountable in the same way. Others could learn such responsibility from Adam, and become accountable. The first creation story expresses this human state of responsibility and dominion. This story gives it specific form as it tells about Adam in the garden. The storyteller notes that God made many kinds of trees to grow out of the ground in the garden. There are two special trees, which will come to symbolize particular stages of human development, located in the garden. One of those trees will be involved in Adam's experience of needing to give account.

Let's take time to assess where we have come from in relation to a scientific understanding of human development. The traditional view has been to see the present account as a repetition of the story of biological creation. I take a different view. This story only lightly makes reference to biological (physical) development. It deals with social or, if you please, spiritual development. There is no scientific evidence to prove or refute this account. Archaeology can tell us about human cultural development, but certainly, it cannot pinpoint moral accountability. This story is the best one I know to give us this information.

Adam could eat freely of the garden's fruit, with one exception. God gave Adam a fateful command that was both bountiful provisions for Adam's needs, and loving restraint for his protection. Adam's protected environment had in it fruit that could incur human death. Adam's obligation was to the garden, to God and to himself. He needed to care for the garden, and to care for himself by obeying God. This commandment was a serious one, as suggested by Wenham.

This command "You shall not eat," is similar to the Ten Commandments. The threat of death is a motive clause characteristic of Hebrew law. Wenham thinks that the language used rules out the idea that the tree is poisonous, and that eating results only in being doomed to die.[87]

Although I agree with Wenham's observation that God is pronouncing a death sentence, there is a different issue here. This issue is God's motivation for pronouncing such a sentence. Is God only acting in an authoritarian way, or is there a good reason for this pronouncement, other than to show who is boss? My theological bias, based on the nature of God as shown in other scriptures, including many of the sayings of Jesus, suggests to me that God's motive must be for Adam's welfare and not simply to enforce an arbitrary rule. On this basis, I contend that the tree was potentially harmful to Adam, even if there were no rule given for obedience.

Think of it this way: smoking is harmful to a young person, whether forbidden by a parent or not. A wise parent would not threaten fatal injury to a disobedient child, but this case is different. Adam is capable of making a decision for an action that will have consequences for the whole human race, since, in effect; he is God's representative to all humans. Picture someone stopping a hijacker before he can take down a plane and a building.

The name of the tree, the tree of the knowledge of good and evil, although symbolic, was also real in Adam's experience. This name has given rise to all kinds of mythical and magical interpretations that may obscure the real meaning. There is no good reason to attribute some magic curse of death to the fruit of this tree. There may have been a biochemical reason for not eating its fruit. Some component of the fruit may have been incompatible with Adam's own biochemistry. Many plants contain poisons, some immediately evident, and others that shorten life after many years. There are common house and garden plants that are toxic. Our world is beautified and enriched by such plants, but they are not food.

There was sufficient reason for this tree to be in the garden, and there was also sufficient reason why Adam should not eat its fruit. It was God's goodness that planted the tree in the garden, and that warned Adam of the undesirable consequence of eating its fruit.

There is also the theological meaning of Adam's later experience with this particular tree. A later account further develops this meaning. Here it is sufficient to note that human accountability involves the ability to make choices. Good is known in making good choices; evil is known in making evil choices. The perception of good and evil is a result of human moral capacity. Adam had this capacity and the occasion to exercise it. The tree was an amoral instrument involved in Adam's choice. It provided the occasion for Adam to choose.

Adam's relations with God provided Adam the awareness that he had a choice. Other humans may have had the same capacity as Adam. Anthropology strongly indicates the basic unity of the human species. Adam likely had human parents, not some kind of half human creature, biologically inferior to himself. However his parents, as other humans before, and perhaps some since Adam, have not had both the awareness and occasion to exercise free moral choice. This is a state of innocent childhood. From an Anabaptist perspective, theologians are quite confused and confusing in ascribing sin to infants. Jesus himself said of children: ". . . it is to such as these that the kingdom of God belongs." Matthew 19:14b.

Genesis is the first account, as far as I know, of a human being in a position to be able, with awareness, to make a morally accountable decision. This is a unique theological position, if not a unique biological individual. This, I believe, satisfies all that the Bible has to say or develop out of the story of Adam. The fact that he stands at the head of many biblical genealogies does not make him the first biological human being, just as Hans Brubacher, of Canton Zurich, Switzerland, eight generation before me, is not the first human. I don't know my genealogy back further than Hans Brubacher, and the Bible simply does not give us the name of an individual before Adam.

"Over against the tree of life, the tree of knowledge raises the possibility of human death. The two trees represent two possible futures: life and death."[88] There is the penalty of death for eating. The meaning is difficult to discern in the light of what will actually happen. "It does not mean 'you shall become mortal' . . . Death as such belongs to God's created order."[89] These comments by Fretheim, here and below help us to understand God's command.

The command appears surprising, but it indicates the important role law has to play as a pre-sin reality. The command is an integral part of the created order. To be truly a human entails limits; to honor limits becomes necessary, if creation will develop as God intends. This issue involves trust in the word of God. Decisions faced by humans concern not only themselves, but have implications for their relationship with *God*. The command involves the visible and tangible. Trust in God shows itself in concrete matters.[90]

Trust requires a relationship. Although the story does not tell us of earlier conversations of God with Adam, they would have been required for Adam develop a trusting relationship with God. It would seem that the whole placement of Adam in the garden, and orientation to life in the garden, with its appropriate care, had to come about through personal interaction and conversation between God and Adam. To my thinking, this requires the physical (embodied) presence of God, as has been suggested above, as an implication of the story with its anthropomorphisms. We will look at this more in the next chapter.

Preparing the Way to Bring Woman Into the Story Gen. 2:15-25

> "The LORD God took the man and put him in the Garden of Eden to till it and keep it. And the LORD God commanded the man, "You may freely eat of every tree of the garden; but of the tree of

the knowledge of good and evil you shall not eat, for in the day that you eat of it you shall die."

Then the LORD God said, "It is not good that the man should be alone; I will make him a helper as his partner." So out of the ground the LORD God formed every animal of the field and every bird of the air, and brought them to the man to see what he would call them; and whatever the man called every living creature, that was its name. The man gave names to all cattle, and to the birds of the air, and to every animal of the field; but for the man there was not found a helper as his partner. So the LORD God caused a deep sleep to fall upon the man, and he slept; then he took one of his ribs and closed up its place with flesh. And the rib that the LORD God had taken from the man he made into a woman and brought her to the man. Then the man said,

"This at last is bone of my bones
and flesh of my flesh;
This one shall be called Woman,
for out of Man this one was taken."

Therefore a man leaves his father and his mother and clings to his wife, and they become one flesh. And the man and his wife were both naked, and were not ashamed." (NRSV)

It Is Not Good for Adam to Be Alone (Gen. 2:18)

Human beings need the companionship of other human beings. Humans are social creatures. We tend to live in population groups. Even fossil records indicate the group character of human life. The account of God's creation suggests a two-sex character (male and female) of human life from its beginning. Adam, having been isolated in the special garden environment, needed a suitable companion. "For the woman to be called 'helper' (*'ēzer*) . . . carries no implications regarding the *status* of the one who helps; indeed, God is often called the helper of human beings (Ps 121:1-2)."[91] "To help someone does not imply that the helper is stronger than the helped; simply that the one being helped's strength is inadequate by itself ... The compound prepositional phrase 'matching him,' כנגדו, literally, 'like opposite him' is found only here. It seems to express the notion of complementarity, rather than identity."[92]

Imagine Eve telling the story of Adam in the garden to her children. She would likely make mention of Adam's lonely state. It is this loneliness that sets the stage for her entry into the story. It gives her life special significance. Further, it is the word of the LORD God that sanctions Eve's own place in fulfilling Adam's need and subsequently her own. There is added drama in imagining Eve's speaking the words:

"... the LORD God said, 'It is not good that the man should be alone; I will make him a helper as his partner.'" (Gen. 2:18)

God Brought Creatures to Adam to Name (Gen. 2:19)

The plot of the story requires that Eve (if she is the storyteller) not discuss animals until this point in the account. She is not trying to give a chronological or even systematic account of creation. Adam's account (if he were the teller of the first story) of creation, no doubt, satisfies her quite well. She, instead, is telling about relationships. At this point she acknowledges that the LORD God has formed animals and birds.

Adam rightly considers these creatures important enough to give them names. He is a taxonomist. This ability to name and place creatures in categories, (cattle, birds of the air, animals of the field), corresponds to the analysis of all creation into categories by God's activity in the days of creation of chapter 1. Eve naturally would learn to call the animals and birds of the garden by the names given them by Adam.

Eve is aware of God's larger purpose in having Adam give names to the animals and birds. The names Adam gives them would likely suggest some characteristic of the creature that impressed him. Some animals were more docile and accommodating to Adam. They fit a category we call cattle or livestock.

But something was still missing. Adam's relationship with all the animals and birds he named is not sufficiently fulfilling.

No Animal Was a Fitting Partner for Adam (Gen. 2:20)

Eve could relish this little drama of Adam's continued disappointment. She would enjoy the way God chose to help Adam become aware of his loneliness. Not the cat, the dog, nor even the monkey, if Adam had them with him in the garden, could be a completely suitable companion for Adam. God knew this all along. Adam now comes to realize that for himself.

The Lord God comes to the rescue. Woman is the answer! Perhaps a dream with sexual allusions was the means by which Adam recognized woman as the suitable helper for himself. I ask the reader not to cry "foul play" too quickly. I will explain how I reached this understanding of the text. Try to walk with Adam and Eve as real persons, with real experiences. Even normal experiences may have symbolic human meaning.

Biblical text can be inspired by God, and at the same time be a human account. This text may reflect Eve's own original account. You may ask how the Hebrew words and grammar of the written text permit my interpretation. Remember that, if the original words were those of Eve that, due to shifts in language, they were not likely the actual words of the present Hebrew text. Most likely, translators and writers sought to be faithful to the account in their use of words for the basis of the Hebrew text in attempting to represent its symbolic meaning. Keep this in mind as we continue our interpretation of this text.

God Causes Adam to Fall into a Deep Sleep (Gen. 2:21a)

The LORD God puts Adam into a deep sleep. "Possibly sleep is mentioned here because God's ways are mysterious and not for human observation, (Dillmann, von Rad), or because to imagine man conscious during the operation would destroy the charm of the story (Cassuto). Certainly the remark about closing up the flesh afterwards must be ascribed to the narrator's concern for the beauty of the occasion." [93] In today's society, the text might suggest the application of an anesthetic-induced sleep before a major surgery.

In Genesis, times of deep sleep result in something quite different from surgery. In Genesis 15:12, Abram had such a deep sleep. In v 1, the story starts with "the word of the LORD came to Abram in a vision." The action of Abram's vision consummated a covenant with God. Jacob, in his sleep, dreamed of a ladder reaching heaven, Gen 28: 10-17. Joseph's dreams are well known, and Pharaoh's dreams changed the course of Hebrew history.

Sleep, vision, and dreams go together. If we take the source of the text back to Adam and Eve, it is easy to see that what is reported as major surgery may have taken place in a dream given by God. The text doesn't say that this was a vision or dream, but it does say that Adam was in a deep sleep. If Adam is doing the reporting, this may be what he saw in a dream while he was asleep. A possible inference is that it was a dream experience, not an actual surgery. It definitely was a preparation of man for relationship with woman and married life.

Adam's Sleep Vision (Gen. 2:21b)

The taking of the rib or part of the side is highly symbolic, and is often given such meaning in sermons. "Indeed, the whole account of woman's creation has a poetic flavor: it is certainly a mistake to read it as an account of a clinical operation or as an attempt to explain some feature of man's anatomy (cf. von Rad, Procksch). Rather, it brilliantly depicts the relation of man and wife."[94] My dream interpretation attributes this brilliance to God who gave the dream, not to the storyteller.

"The rib is only one step removed from the dust, and hence stresses common ultimate origins, but the different image may reflect differences in design (no known ancient parallel exists for the separate creation of woman)."[95]

God Brought the Woman to Adam (Gen. 2:22)

"God designs and builds [בנה *bānâ*] woman out of already existing material. This image may be compared to that of the potter who both designs and fashions an object . . . . Unlike the dust, the rib is living material. The theological force of this creation is implied in 1:26-27–namely, the explicit equality of man and woman in the image of God (being created first or last remains immaterial)."[96] Fretheim further explains this theology:

"Just as the rib is found at the side of man and is attached to him, even so the good wife, the *rib* of her husband, stands at his side to be his helper-counterpart, and her soul is bound up with his (Cassuto, 134)." . . .

Mathew Henry's comment comes closer to the spirit of the text. "Not made out of his head to top him, not out of his feet to be trampled upon by him, but out of his side to be equal with him, under his arm to be protected, and near his heart to be beloved."

Charming as this picturesque tale is, it should be borne in mind that it has a more serious purpose than entertainment. Here the ideal of marriage as it was understood in ancient Israel is being portrayed, a relationship characterized by harmony and intimacy between the partners. [97]

There is poetic imagery and theological meaning in the action of God in the making of woman, but there is a scientific problem for those who take it literally. Preparing a 100-pound woman from a one-pound rib defies conservation of mass/energy, or else God is taking matter from somewhere else, or creating it from nothing. You wouldn't believe me if I told you that I had prepared a kettle of spaghetti from a pinch of salt. Something else is going on here. If mass would not be increased, the woman would have been the size of a tiny baby, likely premature birth size. Biblical scholar Eugene Roop, in the *Believers Church Bible Commentary, Genesis*, has this to say:

Community, 2:18-25. Besides a fertile environment and freedom, God provides for community for the human creature. This section begins with a second speech from God: *It is not good that a person should be alone* (v.18). Because in Genesis 1 we listened to the repeated refrain, *And God saw that it was good*, the *not good* of this speech stands out sharply. After providing a garden and granting freedom, still one problem must be solved–loneliness. . ..

God forms animals. Perhaps they will solve the problem of human loneliness. The animals are brought to Adam for a response. The person names the animals, thereby giving them a place in the world.. Although these creatures were *made of earth* like the human creature, the animals cannot fulfill humanity's need for community. (vv. 19-20).

The tale, using a series of verbs, slows down at this point: *caused a deep sleep ... took ... closed ... made ... brought* (v. 21). The tone is private and mysterious. Out of this mystery, a surprise emerges: a woman alongside a man. Through poetry, covenantal language, and sexual imagery, the text gives voice to the joy of community. *This at last is bone of my bones* ... (v. 23). The human community is formed (2:25).[98]

Sexual Imagery in Adam's Dream

This commentator also notes sexual imagery. The word for flesh, Hebrew *basar*, is translated by the NIV in Ezekiel 23:20 as genitals, and the comment 'clings to his wife,' suggests sexual relations. The word for rib, Hebrew *tsela,* is most frequently translated side or side chamber. The word for made, Hebrew *bānâ,* is usually translated build or build up, but can mean set or set up or even obtain children. The word for take (took, taken), Hebrew *laqach,* is often translated as take, but can also be translated to mingle, enfold, or even marry. There are lots of possibilities for sexual allusions here. The traditional rib interpretation does not do full justice to what may have taken place (how it was understood at first), or how we should understand it today.

If you really think about it, what has this account given us to gloat about? We are humans, made from humus. It sounds better to be a frog, made from a tadpole, than to be a man made out of mud. The male chauvinist gets the ultimate put-down, being a clod, while the female is at least made from Adam, human stock. Lest feminists gloat too much, both are just one short step back to dirt. It is not the material used for creation nor the relatedness or unrelatedness to animals, but the relationship with LORD God, *Yahweh Elohim,* which gives special significance to Adam and Eve.

Bone of My Bones and Flesh of My Flesh (Gen. 2:23)

Adam's own fully conscious statement of the meaning of this experience is given by the well-known pronouncement: "This at last is bone of my bones and flesh of my flesh; this one shall be called Woman, for out of Man this one was taken." v 23 Adam probably observed animals in sexual union. He knew that humans were both male and female. He may have been separated from his biological parents before he had developed a complete understanding of human sexuality. Alone in the garden, he was probably not stimulated as to the function and implication of his own maleness.

To Adam, a part of his own apparent bone and flesh had a new meaning; the meaning of which he only knew because he felt that this female had been joined to him. He considered her as part of himself, a creature of equal nature and value to himself. In a moment, he recognized this as God's answer to his aloneness. Even the English word "woman" carries something of the Hebrew sense of word play used for the two sexes in its ending, "man." A sense of fit between the two is being conveyed, as it must have been in Adam's own words, pronounced to the woman and to God. Note that I am attempting to preserve a literal experience, with symbolic meaning, in a literary work. Note also Wenham's explanation below.

"The first three lines are a poetic formulation of the traditional kinship formula. For example, Laban said to his nephew Jacob, "you are my bone and my flesh" (29:14; cf. Judges 9:2; 2 Sam 5:1; 19:13-14 [12-13]). Hebrews spoke of their relatives as their 'flesh and bone.' It is often suggested that the story of woman's creation from man's rib illustrates the meaning of this traditional kinship formula. "The first man could employ . . . (these) words in their literal connotation: actually bone of his bones and flesh of his flesh!" (Cassuto, 1:136). This formula sets man and woman on an equal footing as regards their humanity, yet sets them apart from the animals." (vv 19-20; cf. 1:26-28).[99]

If one takes this story as an old tradition dating from Adam and Eve, then the traditional Hebrew kinship expression may be evidence of a common awareness of the story and usage of terminology among the descendants of Adam and Eve.

No Shame in the State of Marriage (Gen. 2:24-25)

It is not clear whether the statement regarding no shame in marriage is one Eve would have added to her story or a later addition by another, to add clarity to the meaning of the story. Eve may have supported this concept, and God could have prompted its addition for those not sufficiently aware of the implication of Eve's story.

The pronouncement regarding no shame in marriage is a theological conclusion that sanctions marriage and sexual union between one man and one woman. It also supports the formation of a new social unit, apart from the family of origin. It may be a way of saying that it is necessary for a son to leave home, as well as the more readily accepted leaving of the daughter in many cultures. Fretheim's explanation below is helpful.

One Flesh

Verse 24 stands out from its context by the way in which it makes explicit reference to a later time—namely, when children are born and one can speak of fathers and mothers (the NRSV is more explicit than the NIV). The narrator thereby links God's original intention for creation and later practice in providing an etiology of marriage. The previous verses provide the reason for this practice—namely, a man leaves his parents and clings to his wife. Inasmuch as it was usually the woman who left the parental home, such a departure does not have a spatial reference, but alludes to leaving one family identity and establishing another with his wife. These verses make no mention of children; rather the writer focuses on the man-woman relationship, not on the woman as the bearer of children. God's creation values sexual intimacy as being good. Although the text does not speak explicitly about single human existence, it does not imply that, in order to be truly human, one must marry.[100]

That this couple was naked and unashamed may be a transition to the next story. It suggests that there was a time when sexuality did not carry the tinges of shame that resulted in the storyteller's indirect recounting of the full beginning of Adam and Eve's relationship. It also suggests that Adam and Eve were living in a very favorable physical environment in which they could feel comfortable, or at least not too cold, without clothing. In this way of reading the text, it is an acceptable idea that both Adam and Eve left their families of origin before being brought together by God to form a family unit. Whatever their own cultural heritage, they had a very primitive living situation with respect to clothing.

I have been using the name Eve for the woman. This name does not actually occur until the next section of text. It gives a more personal feel to the presentation than the actual term, woman. Paleontology, archeology, and anthropology show that our species, Homo sapiens, was around a long time before the dates that are reasonable for Adam and Eve.

Both stories give a tradition related to a particular family. The family traced its genealogy back to Adam, as listed in later Genesis accounts. What is so significant about this family tradition is that it is not only a revelation from God, but it is a revelation of God. God is the Creator and Possessor of heaven and earth. God is identified this way, by Abram and Melchizedek, in Genesis 14, suggesting that both have knowledge of this kind of God that must come from their traditions. Moses also shows awareness of a creation tradition, when he says in Deut. 4:32, "For ask now about former ages, long before your own, ever since the day that God created human beings on the earth . . ." Abraham and his Israelite descendants had a concept of God as Creator. It was part of their faith, and suggests that they had an account of creation, either oral or written. We cannot specify its full content, but it is reasonable to think that it could have been the primal account that is now the basic source of our present Genesis accounts.

Adam is the first one to receive the revelation of God, and the first one who experienced what it was to know God personally. This puts Adam in a unique role with respect to all human beings. He had an encounter of the first kind, a God encounter. Eve learned about God from Adam, and in this sense was in a dependent relationship with Adam, unless God also mentored Eve, before bringing her to Adam. The story does not tell us about an experience of Eve with God before she was brought to Adam. The garden story indicates that God went to considerable lengths to prepare a setting for a human being's first encounter with God. It appears to be an encounter, at first, with one human only, Adam.

The nature of God, shown by bringing animals to Adam, suggests that God wanted Adam to discover knowledge of the garden world for himself. The acquisition of such knowledge of the world is a rudimentary science. The two beginning Genesis accounts are complementary. The first one shows strong left-brain logical order and structure, but the second is more right-brain, intuitive and artistic. Perhaps the first story bears the mark of Adam, the categorizer of nature, and the second that of Eve, the specialist in relationships. Eve, of course, would be retelling some of Adam's experiences he would have told her. Retelling provides a tool that may have shortcomings, but it does give a new perspective in place of the traditional documentary hypothesis that is being questioned by scholars. In any case, these two accounts are complementary, no matter how they were composed and transmitted to us.

Sister Anna's home, the human touch of order and art

Chapter 8

Adam and Eve Sin

Genesis 3:1-24

"Now the serpent was more crafty than any other wild animal that the LORD God had made. He said to the woman, "Did God say, 'You shall not eat from any tree in the garden'"? 2 The woman said to the serpent, "We may eat of the fruit of the trees in the garden; 3 but God said, 'You shall not eat of the fruit of the tree that is in the middle of the garden, nor shall you touch it, or you shall die.'" 4 But the serpent said to the woman, "You will not die; 5 for God knows that when you eat of it your eyes will be opened, and you will be like God, knowing good and evil." 6 So when the woman saw that the tree was good for food, and that it was a delight to the eyes, and that the tree was to be desired to make one wise, she took of its fruit and ate; and she also gave some to her husband, who was with her, and he ate. 7 Then the eyes of both were opened, and they knew that they were naked; and they sewed fig leaves together and made loincloths for themselves.8

They heard the sound of the LORD God walking in the garden at the time of the evening breeze, and the man and his wife hid themselves from the presence of the LORD God among the trees of the garden. 9 But the LORD God called to the man, and said to him, "Where are you?" 10 He said, "I heard the sound of you in the garden, and I was afraid, because I was naked; and I hid myself." 11 He said, "Who told you that you were naked? Have you eaten from the tree of which I commanded you not to eat?" 12 The man said, "The woman whom you gave to be with me, she gave me fruit from the tree, and I ate." 13 Then the LORD God said to the woman, "What is this that you have done?" The woman said, "The serpent tricked me, and I ate." 14 The LORD God said to the serpent,

"Because you have done this,
cursed are you among all animals
and among all wild creatures;
upon your belly you shall go,
and dust you shall eat
all the days of your life.
15 I will put enmity between you and the woman,
and between your offspring and hers;
he will strike your head,
and you will strike his heel."

16 To the woman he said,

"I will greatly increase your pangs in childbearing;
in pain you shall bring forth children,
yet your desire shall be for your husband,
and he shall rule over you."

17 And to the man he said,

"Because you have listened to the voice of your wife,
and have eaten of the tree
about which I commanded you,
'You shall not eat of it,
cursed is the ground because of you;
in toil you shall eat of it all the days of your life;
18 thorns and thistles it shall bring forth for you;
and you shall eat the plants of the field.
19 By the sweat of your face
you shall eat bread
until you return to the ground,

for out of it you were taken;
you are dust,
and to dust you shall return."

20 The man named his wife Eve, because she was the mother of all living. 21 And the LORD God made garments of skins for the man and for his wife, and clothed them. 22 Then the LORD God said, "See, the man has become like one of us, knowing good and evil; and now, he might reach out his hand and take also from the tree of life, and eat, and live forever" 23 Therefore the LORD God sent him forth from the garden of Eden, to till the ground from which he was taken. 24 He drove out the man; and at the east of the garden of Eden he placed the cherubim, and a sword flaming and turning to guard the way to the tree of life." *NRSV*

Chapter 3 of Genesis is part of the larger story that both precedes and follows it, as discussed by Fretheim:

"This chapter does not stand isolated. It has long been recognized as an integral part of the story from 2:4 to 4: (24). Some scholars have suggested that the story had an earlier form, particularly in view of the trees (see p. 350), but no consensus has emerged. Given the high value this text has had through the centuries, the reader may be surprised to learn that the OT itself never refers to it (Eden is mentioned in 13:10; Isa 51:3; Ezekiel 31:9, 16, 18; 36:35; Joel 2:3). The closest parallel to the story is Ezekiel 28:11-19, a lamentation over the king of Tyre: "you were in Eden, the garden of God . . . were blameless in your ways from the day that you were created, until iniquity was found in you . . . and the guardian cherub drove you out" (vv. 12, 15-16). Ezekiel 28 however, includes no mention of prohibited trees, the serpent, eating or cursing the ground. . . . Unlike the Mesopotamian parallels, this story develops a sharp sense of human responsibility for the disruption of God's good creation.[101]

Independent and Irresponsible Conversation (Gen. 3:1-5)

Roop list some things the text does not say, since readers may be influenced and confused by past interpretations. 1. The word "Fall" does not appear and "disobedience" would seem more apt than more theological words such as "sin" and "Fall." 2. There is little information about the serpent, but it is considered '*ārûm*, which, in Proverbs, is often the opposite of foolish or simple. The snake is a creature like others, but is a bit more astute. 3. The story doesn't tell us why the conversation happened between the snake and the woman, rather than between the snake and the man. Hebrew narratives normally have two actors "on stage," and the snake and the woman are these two.[102] Nor does the story say that the snake had legs but lost them, although some may read such an interpretation into this from the curse ". . . upon your belly you shall go."

Comments by Fretheim help us to see both the story and its meanings:

Much debate has centered on the identity of the serpent. While the Old Testament has no interest in this question, the situation changes in the inter-testamental period. The association of the serpent with the "devil" in Wisdom 2:24 (see Rev 12:9; 20:2) has enjoyed a long history. While this interpretation may be a legitimate extension of the relationship between the serpent and temptation . . . the text does not assume such metaphysical considerations.

The text does not focus on the serpent per se, but on the human response to the possibilities the serpent presents. As such, the serpent presents a metaphor, representing anything in God's good creation that could present options to human beings, the choice of which can seduce them away from God. The tree itself becomes the temptation, while the serpent facilitates the options the tree presents.[103]

Can a Snake Talk?

A scientific issue is whether a snake is talking with a human voice. This is not an issue that most Bible commentators would even consider. For many, the story has metaphysical meaning, and is not an actual account. For others, if the Bible says it, they believe that is the way it happened, and that it should not be questioned. But if the story is for real, which would be my approach, without suggesting miraculous interpretations, the question regarding the snake's voice is unavoidable. The word for snake or serpent is Hebrew *nachash*[104]; which is *Strong's "OT:5175 nachash (naw-khawsh'); from OT:5172; a snake (from its hiss). . ."*[105] This may suggest the hissing sound that some snakes make. Snakes are not equipped with vocal abilities needed for complex speech. We should ask ourselves how a primitive person would express ideas that were evoked by the presence of a snake in the human mind. Picture the woman in the garden. Note that this account begins with an evaluation of the nature of the snake as crafty. A snake may often have appeared quite unexpectedly. Its mode of locomotion would have been puzzling. It appears that the storyteller credits it with a nature of sly wisdom, perhaps a trait appearing desirable to the woman.

Eve may have suddenly spied the serpent coiling about the tree, eating the forbidden fruit. The thought would have crossed her mind, "Did God really say, 'you must not eat. . .'" To tell someone else what happened would present a dilemma. Was this her questioning idea, or did it come from the snake? Also keep in mind that the Genesis account is inspired by God. Is the temptation to sin innate to the woman, or is it most properly stated as coming from a source other than the woman? The issue is a theological one, more than a scientific one. The simple solution is to represent words as being spoken by the serpent. Having the serpent speak also creates a symbol carrying the theological meaning that temptation comes from source other than human beings in this story. Wenham helps us explore the larger context and background of the story's present form in his comments below.

"But as Westermann observes, it hardly seems likely that Genesis 3 would have mentioned the LORD God's creating the snake if it was supposed to represent the archenemy of the true faith. It has also been pointed out that in the ancient Orient snakes were symbolic of life, wisdom, and chaos (K. R. Joines ZAW 87 [1975] 1-11, all themes that have points of contact with the present narrative, though whether this is sufficient explanation of a snakes presence here is doubtful. It may be that we have here another transformation of a familiar mythological motif. The Gilgamesh Epic relates how Gilgamesh found a plant through which he could avoid death. Unfortunately while he was swimming in a pond a snake came out and swallowed the plant, thereby depriving him of the chance of immortality. Here in Genesis we have quite a different story, but once again a snake, man, plants, and the promise of life are involved, though here man loses immortality through blatant disobedience, whereas in the epic that loss seems to be just a matter of bad luck."[106]

It is reasonable to think that such symbolism grows out of a common cultural experience, which could well be an actual experience of common ancestors. That some have distorted the story, and that it lost its true meaning, is a ready conclusion. This is especially true since the altered story denies human accountability and disobedience. The naming of God in the story is instructive, as discussed by the following commentary by Wenham.

"On the basis of the examination of twenty examples of the use of "Yahweh Elohim" in Genesis 2-3 and its sixteen occurrences elsewhere in the Old Testament, L'Hour argues that the Yahwistic author has deliberately used this form to express his conviction that Yahweh is both Israel's covenant partner and the God (Elohim) of all creation. Other early examples of its use (Exodus 9:30; 2 Samuel 7:25; Psalms 72:18; 84:12) all seem to be making this point. This is most obvious in Exodus 9:30, where the seventh plague of hail is designed to prove to Pharaoh that Yahweh is not merely Israel's national deity but the sovereign God who controls all creation. It is because "Yahweh Elohim" expresses so strongly the basic Old Testament convictions about God's being both creator and Israel's covenant partner that the serpent and the woman avoid the term in their discussion. The god they are talking about is malevolent, secretive, and concerned to restrict man: his character is so different from that of Yahweh Elohim that the narrative pointedly avoids the name in the dialogue of 3:1-5. L'Hour's theory is not completely new (cf. Delitzsch, Cassuto, Westermann, and E. Haag), but he has given a more convincing justification for it than any previous writer."[107]

We need not conclude that the snake was talking with a human voice or even that the woman was responding out loud with spoken words to answer. Later the story tells us that her husband was with her. His response to God's question gives no indication of his having heard a conversation between the woman and the snake.

The woman's first responding thought recognizes the bountiful provision of God. Second thoughts confirm restrictions to eating this particular fruit. A third thought may even magnify the restriction to

"... not touch ...", and finally consider the consequence of death. Then the consequence of death is questioned. It follows logically if the woman is watching the snake eat the fruit with no apparent harm. "A serpent, one of the 'wild animals' (Genesis 3:1), challenges God's warning. (Did Eve see the serpent in the tree eating the fruit without suffering dire effects?)"[108] Further, the snake has sly wisdom, so the woman may well wish to be like the snake. The woman likely already knew the tree as "the tree of the knowledge of good and evil." If God gave this name to the tree, God must have known its meaning. It is reasonable that the woman might expect to acquire knowledge like God's by eating the fruit. Her eyes had to be open to see the snake, now perhaps her eyes could be opened in a new way. The temptation and the woman's own thinking become intertwined.

What would Eve understand about death? If, as some hold, there was no physical death until the full outcome of this incident, she would have no basis for understanding the meaning of death. It appears that she did understand, and her further conversational thoughts show that she came to question that death would be the outcome of her eating of the forbidden fruit. Our past presuppositions may depart from the simple facts of the story, and from a scientific understanding.

Eden may have been a special environment in which death was not as evident as it generally is in nature. The possibility of incurring death must have had meaning to Adam, who likely was the first to receive the initial warning from God. God's command speaks of possible death. God is not communicating without considering Adam's ability to understand. This is not to say that Adam didn't gain a new understanding of death in his subsequent experience.

The great bulk of fossil record is an account of death in nature. This kind of death preceded Adam. It seems unlikely that Adam would have become an adult without being exposed to biological death. However, Adam may have had the potential of eternal life. To me the tree of life is symbolic of the possibility of life without death. This additional experience of life was potentially available to Adam in the garden. This may have been the first time a human being had the possibility of eternal life, which is symbolized by the tree of life. Any thought of Adam being created with eternal life, and of physical death being unknown in nature, until Adam incurred death, is speculation counter to the overwhelming evidence of natural history. Nor is such an idea supported by the present text that suggests Eve's anxiety about death, as discussed by Fretheim below.

"The woman's reasons are likely revealed in the serpent's reply, which focuses on the cause of death. The reference to touching reveals a key vulnerability—namely, anxiety about death. She exaggerates, because she wants to avoid death at all cost. The exaggeration offers evidence of reflections that the woman or perhaps the man have had about the prohibition.

The serpent responds (vv. 4-5) to the point of exaggeration and vulnerability, and with a promise that the humans will not die. This response could be a contradiction of what God has said. But it may be more subtle than that. In 3:22, 'God recognizes that they could eat and not die, *if* they eat of the tree of life.' Expulsion from the garden allows for death to occur."[109]

Thinking and Acting for One's Self (Gen. 3:6-7)

While Genesis 2 shows a God who generously provides, this caring nature of God is now reexamined with a shift of emphasis to a God who withholds. This shift is reinforced by a restriction God has not made, with the phrase, *neither shall you touch it*.[110] Also, the tree is seen as a source of wisdom, rather than God or the "fear of the Lord" being the source of wisdom.[111] The disobedience that follows results, in part, from a distorted concept of the nature of God.

The woman builds the case for eating the fruit in her own mind, and acts upon it. She appears to accept the deceptive logic of her thoughts, and acts on what she has concluded to be true. Eve was deceived or, putting it bluntly, duped by this reasoning. In the New Testament, Paul suggests this as well, and he also implies that Adam was not deceived (1 Timothy 2:14). She gives some of the fruit to her husband, and he eats. His reasons for eating are not given, but he deliberately disobeys. He may have acted out of deference to his wife. Later in the story, he blames her. It seems that Paul is harder on Adam, in his analysis of the transgression, than he is on Eve. Paul appears to attribute sin's entry into the world directly to Adam, not to Eve. (Romans 5:12). Adam makes his own decision apart from the stated will of God. For both Adam and Eve, it is an independent, irresponsible assertion of personal freedom, as suggested by Fretheim below.

"The command seems to forbid an immediate acquisition of knowledge, though without suggesting that humans should not have wisdom. The issue *involves the way in which wisdom is gained*. The fear of the Lord is the beginning of wisdom (see Rom 1:20-21). By using their freedom to acquire wisdom in this way, they have determined that the creational command no longer applies to them. The command refers primarily, not to the intellect, but to success in making decisions in life—true wisdom involves knowing good and evil, the discernment of what is one's own best interests (see 2:9). What it means can be seen from the result. Only God has a perspective that can view the created order as a whole; human beings (even with their new knowledge) will never gain that kind of breadth, for they make their decisions from within the creation." [112]

The woman is expecting "her eyes to be opened," to be like God, in knowing good and evil. She may begin a conversation with her husband about how they are or aren't like God. The outcome of all this was the realization that they were naked. This may have made them ashamed because of an awareness that their uncovered bodies were not like God. What concept they may have had about the form of God, and the nature of their interaction with him, will be discussed below. There is no indication that their shame came from being exposed to each other or having had sexual relations with each other. Their fig leaf job may have been a cooperative undertaking, but it did nothing to cover their inner shame. Fretham points out that how they view the world has changed.

"They see the world differently, *from a theological perspective*. They realize that having to decide for themselves, what is in their best interests, makes everything looks somewhat different. Having decided to be on their own, they see the world through their own eyes. They operate only out of their own resources."[113]

What Has Been Gained? What Has Been Lost?

It is necessary to look more penetratingly at what has been done, and what happened with the inner life of the actors. What has been gained, and what has been lost? Kraus notes that there are many different interpretations of the "original sin." Some see it as sexual enticement and indulgence; while others see it as resentment of God's limitation of their choices. A few, including Kraus, a professor of religion and missionary, relate it directly to the dilemma of human technology being viewed as a solution to the human problem.[114]

Early church fathers such as Augustine, who associated sexuality with this "Fall from original righteousness," reflect the prejudices of their culture and age, which inflated the significance of physical experience and overrated the value of asceticism. However, the Hebrew concept of knowledge, while including sexual knowledge, is much more general, and suggests cleverness and becoming aware. Neither is limited to the dawning of moral awareness.[115]

Another traditional theology thinks of Adam and Eve as perfect; morally, intellectually, and spiritually. Eve, as the weaker, is tempted to doubt God's goodness, and becomes the transgressor. Kraus questions whether this is this the best reading of the story:

"While this is not an impossible reading of the story, it fails to recognize the nature and ambiguity of the temptation and the resultant human situation. In the ancient world, the serpent was a symbol of both beneficial and harmful powers . . . In Egypt, the serpent was a divinity of fertility—probably its origin as the medical symbol. The spreading cobra head was a symbol of the Pharaoh's crown, which suggests a symbol of authority and power.

Among Canaanites, the serpent was worshipped as a goddess who could cause both harm and blessing. . . . Thus, clearly, the serpent does not symbolize a sinister, immoral creature, but precisely one that fits with our categories of pragmatic, practical, clever, ambiguous, looking out for oneself. It subtly twists God's warning and suggests that God is afraid that they will join the divinities that compete with divine power."[116]

As the wife and manager of the household, Eve had daily tasks of food preparation and homemaking. In agrarian peasant societies, this gives the woman control over resources and decisions. The good food and decorative qualities of the fruit would improve her skills and enhance her livelihood ("would make her wise/clever"). This is the same language of everyday modern technology. "The account seems to make a special point of the humans' nakedness, which I understand to be their vulnerability. Adam and Eve were vulnerable and naïve, 'innocent', in the sense of inexperienced. . . . Theirs is a simple, idyllic agricultural existence . . . In such an original condition: they were unaware of their 'nakedness.'"[117] Kraus further expands this thought:

"In this setting, the serpent promises, "I can give you the kind of knowledge that will allow you to control and 'develop' your primitive existence." In Hebrew, the words *naked* and *crafty* form a kind of pun, suggesting that the humans lacked what the serpent had. Technical know-how could expand and enhance their primitive existence. They would not be at the whim of God (nature?) to supply their everyday needs. By implication, the knowledge offered them by the serpent represented a managerial opportunity for controlling and fulfilling life's meaning—the achievement of the "image of God"—by their own inventive skill. The temptation was to take control of their lives beyond, and in disregard of the limitation the Creator had placed on them. This kind of practical knowledge the serpent offered them was not wrong, in itself. Indeed, as we have seen, God's mandate implied the need for such knowledge, but the serpent represented technological knowledge and skill as the means to achieve the true end of life, apart from dependence on the Creator."[118]

Most of what Kraus proposes in regard to Eve is acceptable, but I would also accept the more traditional Pauline understanding that it was Eve, not Adam, who was deceived. She believed the tempting thoughts she experienced, whatever their source. It is not clear what Adam was thinking, only his actions are known from the text. He ate the fruit handed to him by Eve. It could even be that he didn't think twice about the matter, but simply disregarded the command that God had given him. In this case, Eve's transgression appears more excusable, in that she was misled. Adam, in the same way as later told in the story of Esau (Genesis 25:34) "despised his birthright," and became the image bearer of human sin by giving no thought to his responsibility toward God. Adam failed in obedience and leadership, even if he was not deceived.

The human mind is not a "blank slate," nor is the mind's strength or its problem a "ghost in the machine," as defined by Steven Pinker. We exercise our own innate wills and choices. "I do not claim to have solved the problem of free will, only to have shown that we don't need to solve it to preserve personal responsibility in the face of increasing understanding of the causes of behavior."[119]

Unlike Pinker, I argue that our ultimate accountability is to God, although I would not try to refute that a sense of morality has evolved. "The brain may be a physical system made of ordinary matter, but that matter is organized in such a way as to give rise to a sentient organism with a capacity to feel pleasure and pain. And that in turn sets the stage for the emergence of morality."[120]

Pinker's Thought Experiment

Pinker proposes the thought experiment of whether we should obey a God who commands us to be selfish and cruel. He concludes that those who root morality in religion would say that we should then be selfish and cruel, but that those who appeal to a moral sense say that we ought to reject such a God's command. Pinker thinks that this thought experiment shows that our moral sense deserves priority. He can only say this in a cultural context that believes that God is good, and has given us a good moral sense.

Ancient gods were selfish and cruel, and those who believed in them often modeled similar behavior. The Judaic-Christian faith established a new understanding of God, as God revealed himself. The ultimate contrast between Adam and Christ is shown by Thomas Finger, in *A Contemporary Anabaptist Theology: Biblical, Historical*.[121]

"Adam transgressed and followed his own behavioral tendency, before his moral sense of responsibility kicked in and made him feel guilt. Jesus, the Son of God in Christian faith, felt great agony as he prayed in a second garden "My Father, if it is possible, let this cup pass from me; yet not what I want but what you want." And he prayed a second time: "My Father, if this cannot pass unless I drink it, your will be done." (Matthew 26:39 & 42)

Paul catches the essence of this difference between Adam and Christ in Romans 5, and uses Adam as the image bearer of sin, and Christ as the image bearer of salvation. "Therefore just as the one man's trespass led to condemnation for all, so one man's righteousness leads to justification and life for all. For just as by the one man's disobedience the many were made sinners, so by the one man's obedience the many will be made righteous." (Rom 5:18-19)

Having a moral capacity and acting on it are two different things. Adam's problem is shown as the story unfolds.

Hearing and Hiding from the LORD God (Gen. 3:8-10)

The text suggests the physical presence of God, making the sound of walking in the garden. This was no incorporeal spirit, or simply thoughts in Adam's mind about the nature of God. The narrative suggests that Adam had a relationship with God, as real of a physical presence as his relationship with Eve. It may be a surprising idea that God made an audible sound by literally walking in the garden; as strange an idea as that of a snake talking with an audible voice. Scientific observation tells us that snakes make some sounds, but can't talk. It is not a scientific observation that God doesn't talk or make a sound. We are able to learn about snakes by personal observation and by reading scientific literature. Our ideas of God come from theology and from reading the Bible, in addition to personal experience. A snake does not have the vocal equipment to make intelligible speech. God is a spirit, but also the creator of the material universe. Certainly God produces physical effects.

Theophany—God Appearing in Human Form

We can scientifically study the results of God's creativity in nature. Nature and God's creativity are not "hocus pocus," but demonstrate consistent principles. It is no credit to God to accept ideas that are out of harmony with these principles. We do not need to hold those who first told the creation story to standards of scientific principles. We judge their integrity within the boundaries of their limited knowledge. If Adam and Eve told the original story, they utilize a forthright honesty in giving an account that incriminates them. They were not trying to give us a scientific discourse on the nature of snakes. Rather, they relate personal experience as they understood it, and as they were best able to explain it. We should not discount the humanity of those telling the story under the guise of inspiration. Neither should we translate a primitive account into a literal mold of representing nature in a way that denies scientific understanding. Doing thus fails to recognize God's consistent action in nature, which forms the basis for scientific investigation.

Most importantly, the incarnation in Christ suggests that God was in human form. Christ appeared in a resurrected body. The resurrection of Christ poses the paradox of an eternal being in the timeframe of the created universe. Such a being cannot be limited to a short time period almost 2,000 years ago, since eternal implies past, present, and future. Perhaps the resurrection fits the scientific concept of Einstein's relativity of time dimension. I suggest that God incarnate, in Jesus the Christ, walked and talked with Adam and Eve in the Garden of Eden.

Other accounts of theophanies–God appearing in human form– are also found in Genesis; Abraham and Sarah's experience with God in chapter 18, and Jacob's wrestling experience in chapter 32. Some interpreters consider this to be the appearance of angels representing God or simply an expression in a non-literal story. Science fiction has picked up the idea of time-travel, which has some basis in relativity theory, but science has not made this a reality of human experience. Under the guise of trying to demythologize and make an account scientifically plausible, we should not confine God to a limited understanding of God's actions in nature. Neither should we apply a less physically direct comprehension of God as the standard for determining what others have experienced. Let us not deny God's palpable presence within the Garden of Eden. Spirit is not less, but more, than physical nature. It was the physically corporeal Christ who said, "God is a Spirit: . . . ." This parallels John Walton's interpretation of God coming into His temple on the seventh day.

A significant change of attitude has occurred for Adam and Eve. It is not God's walking in the garden that was unusual, but the reaction of man and his wife. They "hid . . . among the trees of the garden." The same phrase, "man and his wife," last occurred in 2:25: "The two of them, man and his wife, were nude, but they were not ashamed." A more complete transformation could not be imagined. The trust of innocence is replaced by the fear of gilt. The trees that were created for man to look at (2:9) are now his hiding place to prevent God seeing him.[122]

The LORD God Exerts Ownership (Gen. 3:11-13)

The pair hiding in shame among the trees of the garden were not hiding from some formless presence conjured up in their imaginations. They were hiding from one whose presence they had seen and heard, and with whom they had had verbal conversation. Adam was the LORD God's adopted son, so to speak. Adam's social/spiritual nature had been formed by God. He heard the LORD God call him. He could no longer hide. He answered God, confessing his fear and shame of nakedness that made him so unlike God. This was an intense sense of personal relationship. Although it may blow the reader's mind, this may suggest that Adam interacted with Jesus Christ in a similar way as he appeared to the disciples. Jesus would have been clothed, but Adam and Eve may never have thought about this difference from themselves because nudity was their normal experience until they began to question how they were not like God. This would be an obvious way that they were not like the God-man, Jesus.

"'Who told you . . .? Have you eaten . . . ?' These further questions are not those of an ignorant inquirer. Their very formulation suggests the all-knowing detective who by his questioning prods the culprit into confessing guilt."[123] God's questions (v 11) imply that Adam did not come to his sense of nakedness by himself. They also indicate that this understanding was related to the experience of eating the forbidden fruit. God's subsequent comments imply (if we take this as an actual experience) that all three characters are present to be addressed. This suggests that God came to the very spot where the command was disobeyed, and where the serpent still was in the tree. There is no suggestion of the serpent experiencing shame or guilt. It may well have remained in the tree eating the fruit. God expresses interest in the transgressors and in the instigator of the transgression.

Adam does not say how he knew that he was naked, but responds to God's question about eating the fruit. The temptation came by way of the woman, but Adam ate the fruit. He blames his wife. There may even be some imputation of blame aimed back at God in the phrase, "The woman you put here with me . . ." Adam's response is not truly complete. He has not accepted responsibility for his own culpability, which is the ultimate source of his knowledge and guilt.

God pushes out the meaning of his original question by asking Eve about her own involvement in the transgression. Eve responds to the direct question, as well as to the unspoken one. She tells God that she ate, but that she was tricked and deceived by the serpent. This shifts blame from herself to the snake, but also admits that things have not resulted in what she was expecting.

A Word to the Snake (Gen. 3:14-15)

Now you might wonder if the snake was really the devil incarnate. I don't know of other scripture suggesting this, but only that we are tempted by the devil in our minds.

If the snake was a "good" part of God's creation, and completely innocent as I have implied, why does God pronounce a curse on it? There could be several answers to this question.

God's curse recognizes the change that has come about in how humans, in their guilty condition, will relate to snakes, and to nature in general. The snake that was perceived as wise will now be loathed as a lowdown, dirty creature. It will be hated and killed. The snake's nature has not changed, but Adam and Eve's attitudes toward snakes have changed. A scientific study of snakes recognizing God's good handiwork in nature can result in very different attitudes toward this maligned creature.

God's words to the serpent reflect the blame the woman has already placed upon it. This subtle but good, natural creature becomes the symbol of devious evil that enslaved her imagination, rather than an evidence of hidden wisdom to be discovered. Such a human attitude leads people to violent acts against personified evil, whether in snakes or other human beings. Even in this crushing violence, there is hope. In the revelation of Christ, we discover the evil within ourselves, which nails God incarnate on the tree of crucifixion. Christ's resurrection undoes the tragedy of death, and provides us with hope of eternal life. It is our own sin that must be undone.

The simplest and most direct understanding of the text is to regard it as a statement describing the kind of relationship that will occur between humans and snakes. Snakes will experience crushing blows to their heads. Perhaps God envisions some justice for the maltreatment of his creature in adding that the snake will strike the human foot.

We should seek to further answer God's original question, "Who told you that you were naked?" Theologically, we recognize the "serpent" as a symbol for the ultimate Deceiver at work in the minds of Eve and Adam. This, as already mentioned, is a much later theological interpretation than that of the Genesis storyteller. The Deceiver makes us feel that being less than God is an evil, and that to be like God is something within our unaided grasp. Acquiescence to this arrogance is the source of our sense of guilt or "nakedness" before God.

From this theological perspective we see "evil" as having a personal source apart from God, just as we see "good" as personal in the Creator. The real Deceiver in this account (not the snake) may however not be a new kid on the block. Some of the chaos that God made into the order of the good creation may have been the result of evil. The purpose of the garden setting was to put limits on this evil until human beings could come to a conscious awareness of good and evil. The purpose of the garden was fulfilled. The unfortunate twist is that Adam and Eve sided with the Deceiver, instead of with the Creator. Their story has become our story. Salvation needed to come from a new Adam, Jesus Christ.

Though beyond Adam and Eve's comprehension, or even that of later redactors, there is the possibility of an interpretation of God's final words addressed to the serpent as referring to the death and resurrection of Christ. This could be justified on the basis of inspiration. A long-standing Christian interpretation is that Christ rendered a deathblow to the "Serpent Deceiver" through the resurrection, but received a bite on the foot by the crucifixion. Commentators argue for and against such an interpretation. I will leave it without further comment. The text, although pre-scientific, may be congruent with a scientific understanding of nature. It would be prudent to avoid attributing such an understanding to Adam or Eve, or even to Moses or later redactors. An idea may be here in embryonic form that can only be known by further revelation.

Finally, take notice that God did not question the snake. A snake is part of the natural created order, which is amoral and cannot choose right or wrong.[124] The curse on the snake is spoken for Adam and Eve's benefit, since the snake is not really a reasoning partner in the conversation. We human beings have transformed the biologically good snake into a serpent image of evil. Biologically, snakes have an appropriate ecological niche. The image of the "peaceable kingdom" includes the snake with the child. (Isaiah 11:8)

A Word to the Woman (Genesis 3:16)

The words of God to the woman reflect the blame the man has already placed on her. Man now sees woman as an object to give birth to his continuing life, rather than one with whom he shares a common life. This kind of attitude leads many modern males to subjugate females to their own desires for pleasure, profit or service. Even in this human desire for self-fulfillment, there is the hope that we see beauty in the midst of the pain of motherhood—and that God would send his son, Jesus, who lived to serve, rather than to be served. It is our own selfish shrinking from suffering that must be challenged, to stretch for a higher calling.

Commentators have noted that no curse is pronounced on the woman or on the man, as was placed on the snake. Rather, we hear a sentence that follows God's clear recognition of guilt.[125] The sentence cuts to the heart of what will become Eve's life experience. Nature's evidence shows that the experiences of the mothers, who preceded Eve and those who will follow her, will be the same. Eve, at this point, was not a mother, but in order for there to be descendants in the Adamic line, she would need to experience the process of birth and motherhood. Without this Adamic line of descent, there would be no Hebrew part or Greek Christian parts to the Bible. Though the sentence may seem harsh, it is actually pregnant with promise.

Birth and death are the cycle of nature, throughout the millennia of the fossil record. In Adam's account of creation, male and female humans were given the injunction to be fruitful and fill the earth. Eve's account of Adam in the garden does not indicate that reproduction was enjoined upon the blissful pair. By this time, *Homo sapiens* were widely distributed around the earth. Perhaps the earth was being sufficiently filled or already full enough for that time.

It may have been that if Eve and Adam had attained the experience symbolized by that tree of life that Eve may never have given birth to offspring. Eternal beings have no need of reproduction to perpetuate life, since they continue without the need of being replaced after death. If Eve had not incurred death, there would have been no need for her to experience the pain of childbirth. It is not necessary to interpret God's word to Eve about pain in giving birth to children as meaning that Eve's body was somehow changed in a way that would make birth cause pain she otherwise would not have experienced.

The evidence in this account does not prove that God somehow messed up biology as punishment for human guilt. There is evidence that relationships were harmed, and that these humans would bear social, psychological, and spiritual scars which would result in further damage. Let us not blame this on some arbitrary punishment of an offended God. These humans were morally responsible and emotionally sensitive persons. Their suffering was, in part, self-imposed. Comments by Roop will help us understand this better.

"However we might define what it means to be a woman today, we must remember that motherhood was the basic definition of a woman for those who heard this text in ancient Israel. They observed great pain and danger being part of motherhood. How might this have been understood, when the relationship between women and men clearly was distorted? What God intended as a relationship of mutuality and companionship, was instead characterized by domination. The woman's urge toward the man remained, but domination by the man, not companionship, resulted.[126]

The fact that Eve would desire her husband would not have been hurtful, if balanced by a fulfilling relationship with God. Adam's "rule over" his wife would have been only loving care, had it not turned to accusation and domination. Adam's social and spiritual development, so carefully nurtured by a "father" God, was now marred by Adam's own action. This was the source of negative repercussions for Eve, and too many of her female offspring who have been victimized by men.

This was not somehow a genetic change passed along to Adam and Eve's descendants. The devastation was not simply a less perfect environment either. The problem for all humans, whether biologically descending from Adam or not, is the same. The problem is that God established a perfect relationship between himself and one man and one woman. This relationship was necessary for the fulfillment of human potential. But it was broken. All other humans, like Adam and Eve, have fallen short of the full human potential, with the exception of Jesus Christ. Our relationship with God is imperfect. We all appear to be less than fulfilled persons. This is not God's fault. The ministry of Jesus is evidence that God continues to actively seek a fulfilling relationship with all persons.

A Word to the Man (Genesis 3:17-19)

The words of God to Adam reflect the relationship the man has broken between himself, the Creator and creation. Adam is ashamed to live openly in the presence of God, who sees into Adam's inner motives. This shame causes us to flee from the gardens of cooperation with God into cultivating nature for the good of all, and to eat by our own painful toil until death reclaims our remaining humus into nature. Even as humans toil in order to be able to eat, there is hope. In the gospel of the new Testament, we hear how Jesus, the incarnate Son, waited, like the birds his heavenly Father fed, rather taking matters into his own hands and turning stones into bread. It is our faithless pride that needs to be undone. God's word is personal and prophetic as shown below by Wenham.

Should this word be "To man" or "To Adam." Many commentators believe this is the first instance of "Adam" being used as a personal name; cf. *Comment* on 1:26.

"Because you have obeyed your wife." Note that as in v 14, the causal clause precedes the main clause, emphasizing the relative importance of the former (cf. n. 14.a.). Obeying his wife rather than God was man's fundamental mistake. לקול שמע, literally, "listen to the voice of," is an idiom meaning "obey"; cf. 16:2; Exodus 18:24; 2 Kings 10:6 (BDB, 1034a).

"Eaten." Five times in three verses, eating is mentioned. Man's offense consists of eating the forbidden fruit; therefore he is punished in what he eats. The toil that now lies behind the preparation of every meal is a reminder of the fall and is made more painful by the memory of the ready supply of food within the garden. (2:9).[127]

One need not take God's pronouncement about the ground as indicating that God deliberately made the soil poor and filled with weeds to punish Adam. Rather, the harm to the soil would come about because of Adam's and others' mistreatment of the soil and environment. Adam had lived in an ecosystem especially prepared for him. This ecosystem was but a limited part of the larger environment outside the garden, to which Adam would now be exposed. He would not have the Creator's instruction to learn how to properly care for this more complex ecosystem. Weeds were simply those plants that he would not know how to use, or fit into his primitive scheme of agriculture. Because of his imperfect knowledge of the larger world, his work would become sweaty toil. Adam's own nourishment would be deficient, and perhaps some foods would even be harmful. He himself would return to humus, a subject of the cycle of nature, rather than one who would facilitate it for the benefit of the whole.

There is no mention or hope given of an undying spiritual dimension of man that would live forever. The human spirit or soul, like that of animals, appears to be dependent on the physical body and not a separate eternal entity, in spite of the words by Henry Wadsworth Longfellow, "Dust thou art, to dust returneth, Was not spoken of the soul." The Teacher of Ecclesiastes expresses the Hebrew ambivalence regarding the idea of an eternal soul in 3:18-21, and again in 9:5-6. No claim of continued conscious existence is recognized. The Christian hope of resurrection is a new and different idea from Hebrew thought.

God Cares for Adam and Eve (Gen. 3:20-21)

Adam's death, though tragic, because the garden also had the tree of life, was in part offset by the fact that his wife would bear his children. His biological existence would be perpetuated, even though his own human body would decay to humus. On this note of hope he named his wife Eve, meaning living, because she would become the mother of all his living offspring.

One need not read this verse, as is often done, to mean that Eve would become the mother of all human beings. In the context of

God's statement showing that Adam had incurred death, Adam's naming Eve simply shows his own hope of having descendants through Eve, not his knowledge that the whole human race would come from his wife. There is too much evidence to the contrary to consider Adam and Eve the first biological parents of all human beings. They are symbolic of the predicament in which all humans find themselves. They had the opportunity to write the human story with a different script, a script in which humans would live in a perfect relationship with God.

The words of God are the words of a hurt parent to the erring child. They recognize the pain and poverty of freedoms sought that that can only be bought with the coin of character. Love withholds the prize not rightly won. Love provides a covering that shame can never produce. Love promises future possibilities that present wrong will not deter. God is the God of promises, which cannot be broken.

Banished from the Garden of Eden (Genesis 3:22-24)

Knowledge of good and evil was gained, but at a cost and loss. Roop comments:

"The speech in 3:22 presents some difficulties. God speaks to a group, stating that man and woman have become "like one of us." The reference is likely the same here as in Genesis 1:26. Yahweh sits in the company of other divine beings, for example, angels. God's speech is addressed to that company.

Expulsion from the garden brings us the last of the consequences of disobedience. Because sin has become universal, a new boundary has been given, one that cannot be crossed. Control has replaced freedom. Coercion has replaced persuasion. God's act to withhold the tree of life cannot be violated. Death, however delayed, will come (Coats, 1975). Von Rod points us to an element of grace in this withholding of the tree of life (1973:97). Humanity cannot choose to eat from the tree of life and thus remain living indefinitely. In a distorted and disrupted world, interminable life would be unbearable. In expelling humanity from the garden we experience a God who withholds, but who also provides a tolerable life."[128]

Adam and Eve Sin

Banishment from the garden to prevent Adam and Eve from partaking of the experience of the tree of life was for their good, and the good of others. The sins, mistakes, and wrong ideas of transgressors would not be perpetuated forever. New generations would take the place of failing generations. New possibilities could take precedence over misdirected ways. In the fullness of time, sin would be met by the perfect sacrifice of Jesus, and death would be countered by Jesus' resurrection.

Adam and Eve's Disobedience
Engraving by Dutch Mennonite artist Jan Lukyn (1649-1712)

From a personal standpoint, we humans see death as primarily evil. We may accept it at the last as a release from pain or from a vegetative existence. In nature, death is part of a larger cycle of existence. Leaves fall from the trees, to be replaced by fresh new leaves in the spring. Animals deteriorated by aging are replaced by vigorous young offspring. If aging were not debilitating to the point of death, where could all the following generations find provisions and space for living?

Eternal life is the nemesis of birth. We are not very objective by looking with favor on birth and with antipathy at death. A theological evaluation of death as the fruit of human sin does not apply to nature as we discern it through science. Nature shows the death of all the preceding generations of complex creatures. This is the universal story of the fossil record, which includes the record of human beings and the creatures of their family tree.

Sometimes, death appears to be a gradual or painless slipping from existence. Other deaths are violent or cruel. If what science says about the long history of death is true, we must indeed struggle with why the Creator would have made it part of the scheme of things. Some will say that we must be tough realists, and accept that there is no Creator. Nature is not for our welfare. We just happened to come into existence by the chance processes of evolution. Only we can contemplate the meaning of life, and only we determine its value. This, of course, is contrary to all that the Genesis accounts have to teach us.

Death Because of Sin? Or Death Because of God's Good, Created Order?

The traditionally accepted viewpoint is that in the beginning, there was no death, but that death is a result of human sin. This does not appear to be an acceptable answer in view of scientific evidence. Nor can we accept that, in the end, the Creator is cruel, after all. This would be contrary to Genesis and salvation history. We can recognize death as part of the incompleteness of the present, good created order, just as it was not good for man to be alone.

Humans were meant to be a part of the realization of new life, as symbolized by the tree of life. We can only speculate about an experience in the Garden of Eden that would have fulfilled the meaning of the tree of life, because this is not how the story plot unfolds. Death continues to be part of the natural order. It is Christ and his revelation that brings us hope of resurrection.

The concept of the tree of life makes the story of life a greater drama than the limited view of evolution and bio-genetics would suggest. It is a saga which scientific analysis cannot reveal. Science tells us that the genetic code is an encyclopedic descriptor of living things on earth. For complex creatures like human beings, the genetic code is diploid. There are two strands of DNA, two encyclopedias, if you please, telling the story of our biological composition. This is not to suggest that the dual strands of DNA represent a *yin* and *yang* of good and evil, although they do contribute to sexual differences. Well-functioning or defective genes can be present on either strand of the twisted helix of life's code. With this double provision for our ontogeny, many deficiencies can be suppressed, and better characteristics expressed, although often there is no moral or superior functional reason for which gene of a pair has dominance. Brown eyes are not better than blue, regardless of our personal endowment or bias.

Evolutionary theory and bio-genetics see the possibility of change in living things in relation to this twofold genetic code, and how it is replicated from one generation to another. Some parts of a strand of DNA may simply be chance configurations, with no immediate impact on the genetic story. It is possible that such areas could contribute to some new characteristic in a future generation. However, even if we could recover DNA from an extinct dinosaur, we would be at a loss to determine that it was undergoing changes into a bird. The fossil record does suggest that some dinosaurs developed into birds. We can observe and rationalize such permutations after the fact, but we can only make wild guesses at the direction of natural change. Selection in nature is not like selective breeding with a desired end in sight unrelated to survival, as far as evolution can tell.

Changes in our genetic structures during our lifetime result from degenerative events, such as exposure to radiation and adverse free radical reactions. The cycle of birth and death provides for renewal and for change in living creatures from generation to generation, but, as far as we know, does not result in creatures with eternal sentient life. These ideas do not help us determine when humankind gained knowledge of good and evil. Science does not satisfy our need to recognize our moral nature, or to understand the significance of our life and death.

No Genetic Inheritance of Sin

There is also no genetic inheritance of sin, nor is sin a product of the physical environment. Sin comes from a marred relationship with God. We each bear our own responsibility for rejecting God. Wenham suggests that the relationship of Adam and Eve with God is undergoing drastic change.

"It is nevertheless striking that life and death are not mentioned in so many words in Genesis 3:17-19; the return to dust is presented as inevitable rather than an immediate consequence in the death penalty which 2:17 led us to expect. Just as remarks about toiling for food suggest that exclusion from the garden is imminent, so does the ultimacy of death, for obviously man could expect to live forever if he were to eat of the tree of life. It may be then that the narrator avoids life-and-death language in this verse, because for him only life in the garden counts as life in the fullest sense. Outside the garden, man is distant from God and brought near to death. The warnings about returning to dust eventually hint that a drastic change will shortly overtake the man."[129]

Animal life was made subservient to Adam and Eve in a new way. Animals were sacrificed to provide clothing. Skin clothing was, no doubt, common to other human beings. Archaeological evidence shows the use of animal hides for clothing. The naked state of Adam and Eve is not to be taken as the norm for this period of time. Some suggest that killing animals for clothing may have been symbolic of atoning. It is even more poignant to consider the possibility, as suggested earlier, that Jesus Christ is God present with Adam and Eve doing the act of killing animals and preparing garments for the guilty pair. God is clothing them, as it were, with a "robe of righteousness."

Clothing was also necessary to the kind of existence Adam and Eve would experience outside the garden. God was dealing with them in a loving way, preparing them to meet their own needs.

Too much attention to the wrongful acts of Adam and Eve misses the true meaning of the Genesis story. Humanity is not marred by some vicious sovereign's cruel tampering with our genetic composition, or the state of innocent nature. We all are drawn beyond our own abilities to cope, by our own free choice, between knowledge and virtue and power over peace. The result of our free choice is the destruction of our environment and the eventual death of our own bodies. The only difference between us, and those who first consciously made a wrong moral choice, is that we do not have the possibility of lasting physical life in an ideal environment. The Greek Christian Bible reveals that we do have the choice of eternal life through the resurrection. Humans are not condemned by God, or by the acts of Adam and Eve, but by our own actions.

A prevalent theological view of original sin, passed on to all humans as the descendants of Adam and Eve, implies that sin is a case of bad genes, in the modern concept of genetics. If babies are born sinners, then it would seem that we have an excuse for our bad actions. We were not given a choice about who our biological parents would be. We have no moral responsibility for our genetic endowment. We can't be blamed for genetic deficiencies, or boast about our wonderful selection of superior traits. We are simply born as babies, with various potentials and propensities. As we grow, our experiences and our choices contribute to what we become. We do become a battle ground for the tug between good and evil. We as creatures are able to have an awareness of both the Creator and the Deceiver, and are accountable for our choices.

The Eden story continues, with the sinning pair banished from its luxuriant garden. The nature of the cherubim guarding the way back into the garden is likely beyond scientific speculation. I accept spiritual beings as real, if not more real than human beings. Perhaps, however, the imagery of a flaming sword flashing back and forth could suggest the appearance of lightening. Perhaps Adam and Eve fled from the garden in the first thundershower of their experience. Looking back, they may have seen towering thunderclouds lit up by great flashes of lightening. They could have been too terrorized to fully remember the way they fled, or to ever risk going back, had they known where to go.

It was clear to them that they were banished from Eden—to a new and more difficult life which would end in death. Perhaps it was not so much that God banished them from the garden, but that the very moral awareness and experience of guilt God gave them as their human potential which caused them to flee from the garden, where they had experienced the presence of God. Clothing and trees were not sufficient to cover them. They had become terrified of God, who exerted his ownership of the garden for which they had become delinquent caretakers.

In the drama of the continuing story, humans continue to meet God in many places. The whole earth and the universe belong to the LORD God, as affirmed by the first account about God the Creator. God continued to take significant new actions and initiatives in order to overcome the human guilt, which caused humans whom God had created in his image, to flee from God's presence. There have been many revelations throughout history showing God's selfless, seeking love.

It's All Adam's Fault?

The ills of the world and of the human race have frequently been blamed on Adam. God is pictured as one, who for the sake of imposing punishment, messed up his good creation and human biology. Innocent children are damned to hell as retribution for their innate inherited sin. I do not wish to belittle sin or deny the presence of evil in our world. But I think it is more appropriate to look at our choices as free moral beings, and as willing participants in the corrupt social structures of our times, if we wish to deal with the root sources of evil. The story of transgression against God is our story today, and not simply a story placing the blame for our problems on a past generation. Adam and Eve failed to attain the possibilities given them. Their actions affected us, but we also have failed as responsible adults.

The Best Is Yet To Come

Greek culture envisioned a golden age in history past. The picture in our Hebrew scriptures is more complex than that of a highly cultured civilization, from which the present has degenerated. The Hebrew and Christian Bible look forward to a more perfect future, and invite us now to begin living in the light of this coming reality. God's creation was good, but there was room for further development. There was good, and even very good, but better and best were yet to be. Adam and Eve took a step in the opposite direction of God's unfolding plan for creation, but God's plan was not, and cannot, ultimately be thwarted. This was the hope held out to the sinning pair, and it is still held out to us. The question is in what direction we take our lives, in God's or in our own?

God's actions toward Adam and Eve and creation were intended to be redeeming, after these serious missteps of responsible human adults, not vindictive. Those who now would turn the world over to a fiery holocaust of nuclear war do not know the spirit of God. This is not to say that such destruction cannot happen, but that such an end to our universe cannot be God's intent. In the past, judgment came many times through evil means, but its perpetrators were denounced as evil. God's purpose has always been life, not death. Our hope is that God brings life even out of death. Praise God for his unfailing love!

God's Purpose For Humans Continues

Genesis has been misunderstood, and misused in many ways. We should see ourselves as in and of the world that God created; as creators in God's image, ready to continue this good work, in harmony with God's ongoing plan. The accounts in Genesis were never intended as the end or final purpose of Creation or the human story. We are called to be active participants in realizing God's purpose for the world. This does not give us license to be petty lords, greedily grasping nature's goodies for ourselves, with no regard to consequences. We are to be caretakers, as Adam was to be in the garden, and as he was even when banished from the garden, for he was still intended to be a gardener. The difference now is that our labor is often difficult and not always rewarding, and life is finally terminated by death.

The good news of the Christian story is that God has reversed the missteps of those humans who lived in the paradise of Eden. God the father made himself physically present, to toil die alongside, and in place of, this human creature that marred the image of God gave him. God the mother suffered the physical pains of giving birth to a new humanity alongside, and in place of, this creature who wanted to give birth to herself as God. We who grasp for being like God are told the story of God, who relinquished his place in paradise, to take on the limitations of our physical nature, showing us what God's unmarred image really was meant to be. The challenge for us is to willingly move beyond the confines of the paradise we seek to create for ourselves, and to enter into the work of God in a creation marred by human sin, so that God's Spirit can give birth to Christ in us. This new earth will be the work of God. We are meant to work with God.

In the third account of Genesis, we step from the majesty of God in creation, and the wonder of God in relationship, to the agony of broken relationships and the misery of Creation violated. God has not changed in attitude or action of support for the Creation or its erring human creatures. God can live with human inconsistency, and still move toward the next goal of Creation and relationship with humans. So begins the great drama of salvation, and mystery of incarnation.

God is at work in a long story of salvation history. God also works in a long scientific story of creation. The salvation story is preserved in the Bible. The Creation story is preserved in the rocks of the earth and the appearance of the universe that is being discovered by science. Both stories are essential to a fuller understanding of God. However, we do not understand either story by our minds alone, but only by the presence of Christ in our lives through faith. God wants this kind of relationship with each one of us. This story begins in the first three chapters of Genesis, but must continue now in our individual lives. To God be the Glory!

Adam and Eve Sin

The cross decorated for Easter at Immanuel Mennonite Church

Chapter 9

Some Perspectives

We started in chapter 1 with a discussion of the history of the early chapters of Genesis, to help us better understand how to interpret them. By now, I hope we have looked at a variety of perspectives that may or may not help us to understand the truth of these accounts. We will try to see why some perspectives are misleading, resulting in unnecessary pitting of the Scriptures against science.

The Perspective of Biblical Theology vs. Natural Theology

I believe theology should be developed from what we read in scripture in relation to personal experience, and not primarily from philosophical assumptions postulated from the fundamental nature of things. I would like to give some of the reasons for my theological viewpoint, which I admittedly am biased towards.

Our theological ideas develop over many years. We bring our basic theological viewpoints to the reading of the early accounts of Genesis. My own thinking has been shaped in a special way by the Anabaptist theology of the Mennonite Church. The line of study in this book deals with some very basic theological ideas common to all Christians. My intent is to look at the text from a hermeneutical perspective as I have described in this chapter and the first chapter of the book. I believe theology should be developed primarily from scripture. It is there that we learn to know God as a person, and learn what God requires of us. The record of God's self-revelation is in the Bible. Nature reveals God's power and majesty, but not the possibility of relationship with God. I believe theology should be primarily Biblical theology, not a humanistic natural theology.

Natural theology tries to start from some fundamental logical principle and build a complete system for understanding God. This kind of approach has had adherents in the past, but such attempts have eventually been shown to be inadequate. They also seem arrogant. Can a created being somehow outthink its Creator by being able to understand the nature of the Creator? We come to know other persons by what they reveal about themselves, and by our common experience of the human condition. We cannot equate our own human experiences to those of God, but we can know God, as God chooses to reveal God's self. God becomes real in our daily experience as we relate our own experience to what has been revealed in the words and experiences reported in the Bible. Most of all, I believe, that in relationship with Jesus Christ, the incarnate Son of God, we learn to know God in our daily lives through the Holy Spirit. The Holy Spirit comes to us as we are born anew by accepting Jesus' saving grace, and as we learn to live as Jesus lived.

Those who first gave the early accounts of Genesis were not consciously trying to develop a systematic theology. Neither would this have been true of the Biblical interpreters who edited the text found in the Hebrew Bible. They were simply relating their experience of God, or the experience of God that came from their ancestors. They were neither theologians nor historians in the modern sense of those words, but they had significant beliefs that they considered important for future generations. Fretheim makes this very clear in the quotation below.

"Hence, the most basic effect desired for readers is not that they become better theologians or better informed about their history and traditions. The end desired is more deeply religious, namely, that the relationship with God becomes what God intended in the creation. The theology of the Pentateuch is an applied theology; indeed, it may be said that its theology is in the service of proclamation. All that God has done on behalf of Israel is given in such rich detail 'so that you and your children and your children's children may fear the LORD your God all the days of your life, and keep all his decrees and his commandments. . .so that your days may be long' (Deuteronomy 6:2) and, finally, so that God's 'name [may] resound through all the earth'" (Exodus 9:16)[130]

The Perspectives of Science and Philosophy

We looked above at the necessity of understanding who God is from the point of view of God's own self-disclosure. Let's also take a look at the perspective of understanding God's works in creation in relation to science and philosophy. The disciplines of science and philosophy are human ways of thinking systematically about what we encounter in our experience of life. This ability to reason is part of the image of God in us. For better and for worse, human thought has become more sophisticated, with our accumulation of knowledge. This discussion should help us to find a faithful path, recognizing the development of human thought. I hope to help us in understanding the stories of Genesis in a way that enhances our faith.

Genesis reflects early Jewish faith and culture. One aspect of Genesis is how these accounts relate to the origin of the Jewish community through Abraham and how they relate to the whole human race. Both Jewish and Christian faiths regard humankind as the creation of God. How does this belief relate to current findings of science in regard to human origins and the biogenetic relation between humans and animals? Both faiths affirm that there is more to the meaning and value of human life than is disclosed by our physical and biochemical commonalities with the great apes. Genesis provides a basis for understanding our human condition, and what it means to live in the global community at this point of history.

I choose to bring a realist philosophy to an understanding of science and faith. Our perceptions as interpreted by science give us a growing awareness of the world as it really exists. This world is not an illusion of our minds. There still is the mystery of unknowns, but we can know the world. We can also know God. God is more than an emotional experience in our brains, or worse, simply a delusion from which we need to be freed. Nor is God something in which all take part in some mystical reunion after death. Andrew Moore, in

Realism and Christian Faith: God, Grammar, and Meaning, helps our understanding of this issue.

"Christian realism can be faithfully construed as God's conforming human words to his 'world', and the world to his word."[131] We need to distinguish speech about God from speech about objects that we observe for the purpose of control or prediction as given by Moore below.

. . . when they speak of God's unobservability, theological realists make a category mistake by transferring the 'grammar' of observation in the created realm to the creator. In the realm of created reality with which science deals, the 'grammar' of observation implies practices such as prediction and control, and – if we are realists – the ascription of truth to theories; by contrast, the 'grammar' of theology involves believing and obedience. Thus I shall argue that though there is a sense in which it is proper to speak of God's revelation as his making himself observable, this is not a making visible in the same sense in which electron microscopes make, say, genes visible. The revelation of God is conditioned by his sovereign freedom; unlike a gene, God is not subject to human control."[132]

Our limitation with respect to God requires that we maintain an attitude of humility. David Ray Griffin, in *God, Power and Evil; A Process Theodicy*, indicates the limitations of logic.

"The problem of theodicy, or evil in the world created by God, cannot be solved by logical human reasoning as some may think.[133] We need to receive what God reveals about God's self and the conditions that we call evil. This sometimes leaves us with a paradox not easily solved. This is not resolved by an appeal to process theology. Process theology accepts that God is in some respects eternal, immutable, and impassible (not showing emotions), but it contradicts this view by insisting that God is in some respects temporal, mutable, and passible. Process theologians place stress becoming over being and on relationality. It is helpful to assume that nature is amoral, without awareness of moral distinctions, but that it is being redeemed by a moral God who desires humankind to bring moral criteria to bear in the natural and human realm in which we live."

The creation account of early Genesis should not be read as a scientific document, but it does touch on topics that are part of the realm of science. The basic purpose of the text is to restore our relationship with God, but it does not avoid all concepts relating to science. Genesis cannot pass over all scientific information, when it is clearly presenting a view of the beginning of what we call nature. The idea that nature had a beginning is something that science addresses. I will not deny that there are some issues of contention between the creation account and science.

There is language in Genesis that relates directly to the formation of the atmosphere, continents, and oceans. This does not anticipate or endorse current geological theories about the origin of the atmosphere, oceans, and continents. There are some parallels between how we understand Genesis and how we understand geology.

Genesis clearly opposes atheism, but not the hypothesis that evolutionary processes were involved in creation, as argued by Michael Ruse in *Can a Darwinian Be a Christian?*.[134] The theory of evolution does not require a scientist to be an atheist. Such an atheistic position cannot be scientific. Science deals with the perceptible, measurable realm of matter and energy known through the human senses and with the help of instruments that extend the senses. Concepts of the spiritual are outside the competence of science to discuss. The biological idea of evolution is neither endorsed nor opposed by the creation account in Genesis. Evolution can be a tool that God uses in creation.

The scientific study of the universe and living things is a rightful use of the human mind. While science does not tell us directly about God, it certainly can fill us with reverence and praise for God, as we learn more about the wonders of the cosmos. The physical sciences and biological sciences, rightfully pursued, all attest to the power and glory of the Creator. Knowledge has advanced rapidly in these scientific disciplines. Christians do themselves and God a disservice by trying to use Genesis to support or refute proper science. We should be aware of philosophies, ideologies, and even religions that take on the guise of legitimate science to support their ideas. Unfortunately some of these ideologies may even purport to be Christian, at the same time they distort the truth.

As long as human beings pursue scientific studies, the knowledge of science will continue to change and develop. This does not mean that all we know today will be wrong tomorrow. Truth does not change, but our perspective of truth does change. Much of what we currently believe to be true in science will in the future become part of a larger understanding that reveals the shortcomings of our current ideas. Newton's law of gravitation has been superseded by Einstein's theory of relativity, but Newton's law is still useful in calculations for space travel, even if not absolutely correct.

Creation = Ultimate Causation; Evolution = Immediate Causation

The whole evolution/creation controversy was and is based on incorrect philosophical assumptions by both atheistic scientists and conservative Christians, who fail to distinguish immediate causes from ultimate causes. Mechanistic explanations and scientific theories deal with immediate causes. We could discuss, in detail, the assembly line processes by which a Model T Ford was created. These would all be immediate causes for the Model T, but would not tell us about the man, Henry Ford, the real inventor of the Model T, or about the assembly line that produced it. Nor would intermediate causes give the origin of Ford's ideas and his creation. One could say by faith, that the ultimate cause for the Model T is God, who created Henry Ford. Creation has a lot to do with ultimate causation, while evolution only speaks to immediate causation. Science explores immediate causation, while the basic purpose of the Genesis account is to tell us about God's ultimate causation.

At the point in time of the Genesis account, for example, the flood account about rain presents an immediate cause. These may be simple human observations, only indirectly related to the purpose of the inspired account. Such comments should be taken seriously as coming from a trustworthy person. It is not necessary or proper to always expect that God would keep a limited human being from making a mistake in relating such an observation, which may have little or no bearing on the ultimate truth God is seeking to reveal. For example, when the flood account says only Noah and his family were left, that was their immediate experience. They likely did not know about the global earth and its entire people. It is often a philosophical presupposition related to the nature of the church's striving for perfection that drives such a dogmatic understanding of the truth of scripture. A parallel would be the dogma Galileo encountered which sought to deny his observations of the moon, planets, and spots on the sun.

In other words, recognizing the human part of scripture does not open the door to proving scripture untrustworthy. We consider people we trust to be trustworthy, without needing to have the perfectionist concept that they can never make a mistake. We need to look at what is written from the perspective of the writer of Genesis. This is a good approach to the trustworthiness of what appears to be scientific information in scriptural accounts.

The major problem with what is called "creation science" is not its attempts to rewrite science. Scientists do that all the time as they explore anomalies in their data or theoretical descriptions. This is the very basis for progress in science. The problem is how unconscious that some, so-called "creationists", are of the limited cultural understanding they bring to reading the Genesis text. They believe that science needs to be corrected by what they read in scripture, while not seeing that how they read scripture needs to be corrected. Science may correct inadequate interpretations of scripture. Our hermeneutical approach to scripture should be as thoughtful as our approach to solving a problem in science. Unfortunately for "creation science," such an approach has had no significant impact on science. "Many creation science" ideas have been tested by science in the past and proven inaccurate, such as the attempt to explain the fossil record by one global flood. This kind of thinking shows the reader's need to understand how scripture relates to science.

What we explain as physical mechanisms related to the origin and development of living organisms can never deny the Creator's role in ultimate causation. God can use an apparent natural mechanism to achieve an ultimate purpose. The Christian view of God incarnate in Christ puts him in a position of possible immediate physical causation, like that of a human being. Sometimes mechanical explanations may appear incomplete without recognizing an immediate causation by the Creator, as well as God's ultimate causation. Newton thought God might occasionally need to give planets an extra-orbital push to keep them moving correctly. Later this was shown not to be necessary. Such explanations are now discounted as requiring a "God of the gaps." This characterization seems to fit the ideas championed by "Intelligent Design" theorists.

Part of what I see as my ministry is to make scripture relevant to life in our culture. Scripture can give meaning and purpose to life in relation to scientific knowledge. There may always be areas of tension between our understanding of science and our understanding of scripture. Life is enriched by both studies, and that is how our Creator intends it to be. God never waved a magic wand and filled the human brain with knowledge, obviating the need to struggle to understand the complexity that the cosmos presents to us. Nor did God give us scripture to answer every theological question we might have, so that we would not need to wrestle with where God is in our daily relationships.

God with a Hidden Face

There are hints in the scripture that human beings cannot see God and continue to live. But also has words, metaphorical perhaps, that tell us that someone talked with God or saw God face-to-face. We may believe that God has a hidden face. Abrahamic faiths all maintain that God has made revelations about God's own nature. There are various ideas of how this has been done. Let's examine what the Christian portion of the Bible has to say. Three primary scriptures come to mind. We will take them in their biblical order.

2 Timothy 3:13-17

> "16 All scripture is inspired by God and is useful for teaching, for reproof, for correction, and for training in righteousness, 17 so that everyone who belongs to God may be proficient, equipped for every good work." NRSV

The Timothy passage affirms that scripture is inspired by God. It does not define what particular texts are scripture or how this inspiration takes place. It does suggest that God has a significant role in the origin of scripture, and that this makes scripture useful for exercises that help those who belong to God to do good works.

It would appear that inspiration has a pragmatic purpose similar to that suggested by Fretheim for the Pentateuch, "that the relationship with God become[s] what God intended in the creation. . ."[135]

Hebrews 1:1-3

> "Long ago God spoke to our ancestors in many and various ways by the prophets, 2 but in these last days he has spoken to us by a Son, whom he appointed heir of all things, through whom he also created the worlds.3 He is the reflection of God's glory and the exact imprint of God's very being, and he sustains all things by his powerful word." NRSV

The text from Hebrews indicates that God spoke through the prophets. In other words, God used the prophets to proclaim a message for God, but it does not tell how the prophets received this message from God, or how the text related to the prophets' own thoughts. The "various ways" phrase reminds us of prophetic visions and dreams, unusual experiences, and even a driving sense that the prophet had an irrefutable word from God. For Christians, there is the additional, powerful idea that in our own time, God has spoken through a Son, a very revealing metaphor. This Son is also revealed to be Creator and sustainer of the cosmos. Christians are not talking about a second God when they use the word Son, but are suggesting God's powerful presence incarnate in a physical human body. Whatever one thinks about God's presence and form, we should not set limits that exclude God from being able to be present in the physical realm of space and time. Such thought would displace God from God's own Creation, which is absurd.

2 Peter 1:16-21

> "For we did not follow cleverly devised myths when we made known to you the power and coming of our Lord Jesus Christ, but we had been eyewitnesses of his majesty. 17 For he received honor and glory from God the Father when that voice was conveyed to him by the Majestic Glory, saying, "This is my Son, my Beloved, with whom I am well pleased." 18 We ourselves heard this voice come from heaven, while we were with him on the holy mountain.19

Some Perspectives

> So we have the prophetic message more fully confirmed. You will do well to be attentive to this as to a lamp shining in a dark place, until the day dawns and the morning star rises in your hearts. 20 First of all you must understand this, that no prophecy of scripture is a matter of one's own interpretation, 21 because no prophecy ever came by human will, but men and women moved by the Holy Spirit spoke from God." NRSV

Peter confirms what the writer of Hebrews suggested about Jesus Christ, from his own eyewitness experience. He adds the additional thought that the prophecy of scripture is a direct action of God, through the work of the Holy Spirit. Again, we are not speaking about a third God, but rather as God as physically present in the cosmos through Christ. God is spiritually present in the human mind, giving rise to oral speech, written speech, and God-directed action.

Thinkers of the Enlightenment introduced the word 'nature' into our discussions about the world around us. In some respects, nature is a word that introduces a false dichotomy into our thinking when we separate the cosmos into natural and supernatural as though these make, as it were, two watertight, distinct realms. It is wrong to expect that the work of God is something contrary to the functions of nature in a magical sort of way. Nature may be our human description of how the cosmos functions, but certainly our limited understandings of God's world should not be set up as alien to the lawful regularities we describe in nature. The theory of "intelligent design" accepts this false dichotomy of the cosmos, and appears to exclude God from processes that we describe as natural. It looks for God in the unexplainable and the unusual, rather than in events with immediate, natural, causes.

William Dembski, a leading proponent of this concept, explains and defends this in his book, *Intelligent Design*, quoted below.

"Intelligent design formalizes and makes precise something we do all the time. All of us are all the time engaged in a form of rational activity, which, without being tendentious, can be described as 'inferring design.' Inferring design is a perfectly common and well-accepted human activity. People find it important to identify events caused through the purposeful, premeditated action of an intelligent agent and to distinguish such events from events due to natural causes. Intelligent design unpacks the logic of this everyday activity and applies it within the special sciences.[136]

This is an attempt to set criteria for "specified complexity" and "irreducible complexity" that could only come about by a divine agent. This is a key difficulty with "intelligent design" theory because it looks for the hand of God in that which we have not shown to be an ordered result of natural cause.[137] The Creator should surely be at work in that which we have already defined as orderly laws and processes as well as in those that we have yet to explain. Natural patterns showing design and order come from God. Indeed by the theorems of "intelligent design" God's place in the cosmos can only shrink by the growth of scientific knowledge."

We have applied these concepts in our hermeneutical journey through the first three chapters of Genesis. Christians also have a new way to relate to God through faith in Christ's incarnation. Even this idea was touched on, albeit lightly, in our Genesis sojourn. Genesis is a journey toward the face of God, as revealed in the whole of Scripture.

In his commentary writings on Genesis, Wenham makes clear that many ideas in Genesis 1 are foundational to themes developed in many subsequent Biblical passages as discussed below.

"Any attempt to trace the subsequent use of this chapter [Genesis 1] in Scripture would be most unsatisfactory just because its themes and motifs are so pervasive and its theology so fundamental to the biblical world-view. Here we have some of the principal themes of biblical theology displayed in epigrammatic brevity: there these simple but far reaching affirmations have become the presuppositions of the rest of the sacred story. Gen 1 formed the basis of the first article of the Christian creed, 'I believe in God the Father, maker of heaven and earth.'"[138]

God Revealed in the Bible and Nature

Christians put a high value on scripture, including the early chapters of Genesis. Those educated in the scientific disciplines also value knowledge acquired through research based on empirical and theoretical understandings. A simple comparison of the creation accounts of Genesis with scientific information and theories of origins raises many questions. Commitment to the reliability of both scripture and science leads to fundamental issues about how to resolve the apparent problems.

First, we might ask how and why we understand Genesis the way we do. We should recognize Scripture, including Genesis, as the inspired word of God. The Bible, including Genesis, is also recorded by humans, thus having a dual nature. The written word is not God's transcription immutably preserved. It is in the words of human authors, sometimes spoken and retold many times before being written down. Scripture has been preserved through copying, editing and translation into the form we read today. These writings point beyond themselves to Christ, the fullest revelation of God. These faith assumptions enter into the "how" and "why" of our understanding of Genesis.

Second there are "how" and "why" questions in regard to our personal understanding of scientific accounts of origins. Since science is a human activity, factors of judgment and bias affect objectivity.[139] Science, by definition, deals with observation and measurement of the material and energy components of the known universe; those who say this is all that exists cannot do so on the basis of science. Such statements come from a materialistic faith. Science is directed by theoretical models, often spelled out in the precise language of mathematics. Due to its many successes, some confuse science with authority. Science is better understood as an unfolding of knowledge that is enriched by self-correction, and the development of more comprehensive theories.

Genesis One to Three: Challenging but Essential

The struggle Galileo had in advocating the solar system as proposed by Copernicus is instructive for the need of a helpful attitude that does not pit scripture and science against each other. Galileo said "Both the Holy Scripture and Nature proceed from the Divine Word, the former as sayings of the Holy Spirit and the latter as the most observant executrix of God's orders. . ..two truths can never contradict each other."[140] Galileo appealed to St. Augustine's warning against setting the authority of Scripture against clear and evident reason. "It is the task of wise expositors to seek out the true sense of scriptural texts. These will undoubtedly accord with the physical conclusions that manifest sense and necessary demonstrations have previously made certain to us."[141] These demonstrations are reported by Charles Hummel in *Galileo Connection: Resolving Conflicts between Science & the Bible.*

"Genesis tells us about God. It has to do with theological understanding more than scientific concepts. Those responsible for the present words of Genesis were not scientists in the modern sense. How we understand what happened in certain biblical events might be different had a scientific historian described them. The accounts of Genesis predate the disciplines of theology and natural science. Genesis also represents faith because it cannot be proved scientifically, but this is theistic faith."

I bring understandings somewhat apart from the major Catholic and Protestant interpretations of scripture. My viewpoints have been rooted in an Anabaptist heritage. However, there is no fully developed historic Anabaptist systematic theology. I have been influenced by the Anabaptist, Protestant and Catholic theological thinking of today, consciously or unconsciously. Some thoughts may be my own or at least represent my personal bias.

This study examines problems in relating Genesis and science with the hope of stimulating fruitful thinking, rather than posing authoritative answers. Hopefully, it will be useful to those who care to think about Genesis in relation to geology and other scientific disciplines. It is not intended to be comprehensive or definitive, but rather to stimulate the imagination, and to encourage faith, or at least encourage dialogue between faith and doubt.

A Summary of Findings

The scope of our study focuses on the creation and temptation stories of the first three chapters of Genesis. These stories pose many problems in relation to cosmology, geology, and biology. The later patriarchal stories relate primarily to archeology, and have been explored in some depth by other authors. Some have used biblical stories to conclude the possibility of the real existence of the patriarchs. The people and events from Adam to Noah seem to have a more shadowy reality when viewed through the eyes of science. Some scholars do not grant a high level of historicity even to the later patriarchs, but consider the Exodus story as the first historical event, or the beginning of biblical history.

My assumption is that the characters and episodes in Genesis should be viewed as real, and that careful thinking and imagination can be used to help bridge the gulf of time that separates us from them. We must recognize that the accounts found in Genesis were not told or written in a way that is most familiar to our modern day culture.

God's hand in the Cosmos reveals His power and deity, and God's Word in Scripture reveals His heart in relation to human beings.

Chapter 10

Scripture and Cosmos Reconciled

Background for Conclusions to this Study

I have analyzed the first three chapters of Genesis in the larger context of biblical theology and science, which yield some basic conclusions. My conclusions are basic theological lessons of this study. Many are not new, but have been looked at using a distinct approach. I have interpreted these narratives with the assumption that they represent stories from the life experience of Adam and Eve, which some scholars would call proto-historical (like history, but not written as a modern historian would write with documentation), who were the first known ancestors of the Hebrew people, as well as many other people. Descendants of the Hebrews gave us the Hebrew Bible, and the Genesis narratives. These stories are also symbolic, and carry more meaning than simple narratives about human events. Scholars call this paradigmatic, meaning that they are given as examples, whether true or not. Both ideas are weighed below.

Which view is closer to the Genesis writer's own understanding? Does he offer any clues as to whether he regards the story he relates as merely paradigmatic, or in some sense as a real event in primeval history? The symbolic dimensions of the story linking the garden with later sanctuaries support a paradigmatic reading.... Yet other features of the narrative point in a more historical direction.... For these reasons, I prefer to view Genesis 2-3 as both paradigmatic and protohistorical....It is paradigmatic in that it offers a clear and simple analysis of the nature of sin and its consequences, albeit in rich symbolic language.... But in all societies, and especially the tightly knit family society of ancient Israel, the behavior of parents has a great impact on their children, for good or for ill. It therefore follows that the disobedience of the first couple, from which Genesis traces the descent of the whole human race, must have consequences for all humankind. In this sense then, the story offers a protohistorical account of humanity's origins and their sin.[142]

I accept both the paradigmatic and proto-historical elements of these stories. However, it would be mistaken to think that chapters 2-3 are proto-historical for all humankind. Rather, this is the experience of Israel's ancestors and of the larger clans of which they are only one part. Scientific evidence suggests that not all human beings are descendants of Adam and Eve. However, the paradigmatic aspects of the stories appear to apply to all living people, regardless of biological descent.

God's Power and Divine Nature Revealed by God's World

> "The heavens are telling the glory of God; and the firmament proclaims his handiwork. 2 Day to day pours forth speech, and night to night declares knowledge.3 There is no speech, nor are there words; their voice is not heard; 4 yet their voice goes out through all the earth, and their words to the end of the world. In the heavens he has set a tent for the sun, 5 which comes out like a bridegroom from his wedding canopy, and like a strong man runs its course with joy. 6 Its rising is from the end of the heavens, and its circuit to the end of them; and nothing is hid from its heat." (Psalms 19:1-6) NRSV

> "For what can be known about God is plain to them, because God has shown it to them. Ever since the creation of the world his eternal power and divine nature, invisible though they are, have been understood and seen through the things he has made." (Romans 1:19-20) NRSV

We have considered scientific information, which I have related to the Genesis texts about God's Creation. The passage from Psalms above proclaims that God's power and divine nature are shown in God's handiwork of the heavens. The "world," as used in Romans above, represents the whole created universe, or in the Genesis language "heaven and earth." What Genesis claims is that God is the Creator of every thing. However, the terminology and categories of scripture are simple and primitive in relation to those of current science.

The biblical narratives would need to be encyclopedic to represent the accumulation of human knowledge about the world since the final Hebrew text of Genesis and Psalms was written. Clearly, even the Romans text pertains to a culture, terminology, and time prior to the development of the modern sciences. To force them into a scientific kind of mold would be a distortion. They are quite adequate and truthful for the message that is being conveyed, which is that God is the Creator of everything. However, they do not represent a modern scientific understanding of "nature." The word "nature" is used to represent the accumulating knowledge of God's world as presented by human thought. Our understanding of nature, although far greater than those who have brought us the Genesis accounts, is still a limited descriptor.

Even with these limitations, Genesis tells us much more about God's power and divine nature in contrast to humankind than is told by interpretation of the text of Genesis alone. Nature has existed and continued to change for billions of earth years—not only the several thousand years since Adam. A single human life or the totality of human life is but a drop in the bucket of time. To think of God as eternal is a lot longer to us than could have been imagined by those who have given us the Genesis account. Still, we do not grasp the concept of God being eternal, or even the beginning of God's world, although science has put a number of some 13.7 billion years ago for that beginning.

Heaven, the starry universe, is much larger than the culture of Genesis could imagine. Scientists measure and weigh the earth, even though it may be much larger than those who named it in Genesis could have thought. However, we know it to be a small planet of the solar system, itself only a small portion of a galaxy some hundred thousand light years across, one that is only one of billions of galaxies in the universe, and certainly this earth is not central to the existence of the universe, as might appear to be the case from the Genesis account. This does not make the Genesis account inappropriate, since Genesis is a revelation of God as Creator, and not limited by the changing human perspective of what the universe is like. Genesis is not intended to be a scientific textbook or a revelation about the physical nature of the world. The changing human perspective enhances our regard for the power of God as we begin to grasp something of the nature of the universe being described by science.

Our understanding of the planet earth is far different from that found in Genesis or the Bible as a whole. We have measured its age to be about 4.6 billion years, and the 8,000-mile diameter of its almost spherical shape. We know its composition and shifting plate, dynamic surface floating on a plastic asthenosphere, a very flexible layer of the earth, which surrounds a hot molten core of mostly iron. Genesis doesn't tell us this nor does it intend to give this scientific description. This description, however, enhances our appreciation of the power of God that pushes the mountains up, and then cuts them down to eroded lowlands, which again form mountains as continents collide on their shifting plates. We can hardly fathom a God so great as to do all this, yet this is God's work on only one small planet we call home.

The complex evolution of life on this planet that some Christians get so upset about is similar to the concern of people in the past that argued—from the Bible—that the earth was the center of the universe. The new science perspective, achieved by means of the complexity of biochemistry and molecular genetics, shows that we are a physical part of the whole of life on this planet. We are composed of the elements of the earth, and we are physical creatures who are born and who die in the course of nature. We are creatures of dust and to dust we return, as God clearly stated to Adam.

We are closely related to the great apes, and even closely related enough to mice that mice are used to represent us in many scientific experiments. As such humble creatures, we are exalted as the head of all life on earth, since we share in its physical nature, as well as bear the image of intelligence, moral awareness, and extensive ability to communicate that far exceeds that of other animals. This does not demean us, but helps us to fulfill our rightful place in the world. Our spiritual nature or soul is emergent in our physical bodies which is made in the image of God. Our souls are not eternal like God, but the hope of the resurrection that Christians believe God demonstrated in Christ, gives us faith that we will someday receive the gift of eternal life (remember the tree of life in the Garden of Eden) through resurrection.[143] This view should keep us humble and reverent before God.

Neurobiology suggests that there are many things about our brains that are pre-programmed, and set to function in predetermined ways in the early maturation of the brain. We also may experience behavioral conditioning through early training and socialization. Nature and nurture both influence our behavior, but we still can exercise free choice. This does not eliminate any personal and moral responsibility for our actions.[144] Some parts of our brains even give us the ability to experience religion and have an awareness of God.[145] The study of neurobiology may also free us from some self deceptions, without removing our responsibility to God. In the end, we will know God's power and creativity better, as we understand more of the function and formation of the human mind in the structures and mechanisms of the brain. All truth is God's truth and in the end exalts the Creator. God is acting in the world, though, of course, some people do not agree.

God's Person Revealed by God's Word and Deed

This section considers theological teachings, revealed through God's own word, which is the basis behind the clearly human Hebrew, and English texts we have studied in Genesis. Genesis is a personal disclosure of God's own character and activity. It represents God's personal communication to human beings. Basic to this knowledge is the self-disclosure God has given to human beings who have had a personal experience with God, whose words are retold, written, updated, and translated for us, who speak other languages.

Their words are basic to our development of biblical theology. This is basic to how we know about God, and come to know God in our own personal experience.

God can be known because we are created in God's image with the ability to communicate and to understand communication. God can be known because God has, through personal encounters with human beings, chosen to reveal who God is and what God does. These beginning biblical texts are not full-grown Judeo-Christian theology, but are embryonic beginnings of this theology. There is a progression in our knowledge of God through revelation, just as there is progression in our knowledge of another human being in an ongoing personal relationship.

First, God discloses that God is at the beginning of what is called heaven and earth in Genesis, or the whole universe, in modern terminology. This sets God apart from the created world, with an existence independent from that universe.

God claims to be the Creator of all that we know in the universe. God as known to us is a creator, not a static, uninvolved, unchanging being, although later revelation suggests that God's moral character is unchanging. This gives God prior claim of ownership to the whole of heaven and earth, including human beings. The creative activity of God unfolds over a period of time. There are multiple periods of creation and interdependent activities. Finally, there is rest and celebration of what has been accomplished as very good. But this is not the end of God's creative activity.

God's creative activity takes place through active communication. This has been viewed in the past as divine fiat like that of a King commanding his subjects. A better model would be to see it as information that directs the outcomes of all that God is making.

God's creation of humankind is a special event. God exists in a heavenly court of other beings that are consulted before God creates humans in the image and likeness of divine beings. God alone is God and the Creator of all beings. Humans are created for the special task of becoming surrogates for God in God's created order on earth. Humankind is created male and female, so as to become procreators with God. They are to master these tasks by becoming fruitful and multiplying until they fill the earth and helping it become all that God intends.

Just as later God entered into a personal relationship with Abraham, God chooses to enter into a personal relationship with one man (of many who may be living on the earth at the time), Adam. Adam is the first human being the Hebrew Bible tells us had a personal encounter with God. He is created from the elements of the earth just like all other animals and human beings, with the breath of life. He becomes representative of all humankind. This encounter takes place in a garden especially prepared as a favorable ecosystem for humankind. This human is male, without female human companionship, when God brings animals for the earthling we know as Adam to name. Adam becomes the archetype of the taxonomist and categorizer of nature, but he is lonely. God gives him a dream of a woman created from part of his own body, and when Adam awakes, God has brought a woman to be his helper, companion and wife. Together they are to take care of the garden.

They are aware of this mandate, given to all humans, because Adam first heard God speak this message. Adam knows this because of his personal relationship with God. Eve shares in this knowledge and relationship. They have one restriction in their luxurious garden: not to eat of the fruit of the tree of the knowledge of good and evil, because it brings death. Eve, having been deceived into thinking that she will become like God, eats the fruit, and gives some to Adam. Adam chooses to disobey God and eat, even though he does not share Eve's inaccurate expectations. As they think about what they have done they experience guilt, and realize shame in that they, unlike God as they know God, are nude.

God comes to the garden, and calls to Adam, who responds, then blames his wife, who in turn blames the snake. God curses the snake with a prophetic word that will be fulfilled by the new attitude that Eve has toward the snake. God tells Eve that she will suffer the pain of childbirth in bearing children to Adam who will dominate her. God tells Adam that he will suffer the pain of hard toil in the wider world, where raising food for survival is difficult, and that at last, his human body will return to humus.

God releases Adam and Eve from their failed management of the garden, but provides skin clothing that appears to require that animal(s) die for their welfare. They flee from the presence of God in the garden, and indeed experience what they believe to be an angelic guard barring their return. Likely, they have seen an animal killed by a knife or sword that is wielded by the guardian cherubim. They are kept from the tree of life, for their own good, but due to their own guilt. They represent us all in this experience of disobedience and guilt. Mankind has come of age in responsibility for his own actions.

We are no longer innocents caught up in the amoral processes of nature. We understand good and evil, and choose between them in our actions. The serpent becomes the symbol of the counter pole to God in this struggle. The later coming of Jesus Christ reverses the effect of our wrong actions, and provides, through the voluntary death of Christ, the way of forgiveness for our return to relationship with God, and the hope of resurrection into the realm of heavenly beings, whose image we bear, in full relationship with God.

Biblical history and theology is the story of God's actions, taken to reestablish this broken relationship. God remains the Creator and Owner of heaven and earth. We remain those who are to care for the earth, by mastery of its amoral processes to be used for good in subjection to God, but also in partnership with God.

> "7 The law of the LORD is perfect, reviving the soul; the decrees of the LORD are sure, making wise the simple; 8 the precepts of the LORD are right, rejoicing the heart; the commandment of the LORD is clear, enlightening the eyes; 9 the fear of the LORD is pure, enduring forever; the ordinances of the LORD are true and righteous altogether. 10 More to be desired are they than gold, even much fine gold; sweeter also than honey, and drippings of the honeycomb. 11 Moreover by them is your servant warned; in keeping them there is great reward. 12 But who can detect their errors? Clear me from hidden faults. 13 Keep back your servant also from the insolent; do not let them have dominion over me. Then I shall be blameless, and innocent of great transgression. 14 Let the words of my mouth and the meditation of my heart be acceptable to you, O LORD, my rock and my redeemer." (Psalms 19:7-14) NRSV

> "Then what advantage has the Jew? . . . Much in every way. For in the first place the Jews were entrusted with the oracles of God." (Rom 3:1-2) NRSV

The texts from the second part of Psalms 19 and Romans 3 suggest that the Jewish people were God's agents for us to receive God's word which tells us what God requires of us. We, the children of humankind, can only adequately know God in a relationship in which God reveals God's self by word and deed throughout history. The Judeo-Christian Bible is the human record of this revealed word and deed. It is the source of our biblical theology.

Wisdom/Information Shows God's Hidden Hand

> "Blessed be the God and Father of our Lord Jesus Christ, who has blessed us in Christ with every spiritual blessing in the heavenly places, 4 just as he chose us in Christ before the foundation of the world to be holy and blameless before him in love. 5 He destined us for adoption as his children through Jesus Christ, according to the good pleasure of his will, 6 to the praise of his glorious grace that he freely bestowed on us in the Beloved. 7 In him we have redemption through his blood, the forgiveness of our trespasses, according to the riches of his grace 8 that he lavished on us. With all wisdom and insight 9 he has made known to us the mystery of his will, according to his good pleasure that he set forth in Christ, 10 as a plan for the fullness of time, to gather up all things in him, things in heaven and things on earth." (Ephesians 1:3-10)

> ". . . Book of Life of the Lamb slain from the foundation of the world." (Rev 13:8b) NKJV

The set of texts from Ephesians and Revelation suggest that God had a plan from the beginning of the world. His plan would complete the work that was started in the Garden of Eden, even if in a less than satisfactory way.

It is important that we confront arguments that God's hand is hidden in nature, and that science leads us away from knowledge and dependence on God. Science was pursued with confidence in the western world of Christendom because scientists had an underlying belief that the God at work in the world was a God of order and consistency. Early scientists believed that they were discovering the hand of God at work in nature. They defined laws of nature that showed how God worked. These explanations became so persuasive, that eventually it was thought that God was only needed to begin the whole process, and did not participate in the day-to-day operation of the universe. This was the deistic view.

But it is incorrect to think that deism characterized the majority of Enlightenment thinking. Many scientists and so-called radical thinkers were still basically Christian, seeing God at work in nature.[146] However, God began to be seen as supernatural, responsible for miracles that defied human explanation, and nature was to be seen as the realm defined by consistent laws that often could be described by the language of mathematics. This benefited scientific thinking in that scientists did not write off unknown causes in nature as the hand of God, but continued to pursue research until a logical cause could be found.

Bifurcation of the natural and supernatural is a mistake. This is not because the realm of God that we know as spiritual does not exist, but because God cannot be excluded from the world. We are separate from the realm of spirit, although our emergent spiritual nature can tune in to it. However, God, who created the world, knows the world, and can and does enter the world. God is the architect of the world, the developer of its materials, and builder of its structure. This is the witness of Genesis. God is at home in the world, though not contained by it. The human definition of nature is our map for travel and functioning in the physical world belonging to God. We do not need to show God on this map, because God is everywhere. He is the medium in which ". . . we live and move and have our being." (Acts 17:28a) God cannot be recognized when we confuse our map for the world.

If our map of nature does not show God's hidden hand at work, how can we know that it is there? Genesis suggests the solution in that the world shows the creating speech of God by the information that it contains. In the past, this was thought of as engineering data to be described by scientific laws that simplified nature to a clock-like mechanism. This mistaken view has been ridiculed by those who believed that evolution, as an atheistic mechanism for creation, made God appear to be a bumbling engineer.

God is Not Excluded from Nature

Such critics were already blinded by their assumptions that God was excluded from nature, and who simplified the work of God to have little greater significance than the work of a blind clockmaker. Information found in the molecular, atomic and subatomic sciences provide a different model for how God is at work. God's actions, however, are not confined to a box of our scientific thinking. We do see a great deal of information in nature, but what we see now does not exhaust the information that is yet to be found. God is not hostage to the failure of our definitions of God's work, as might be considered from a perspective of Intelligent Design. God also is not bound by the limited scientific perspectives found in Genesis, as seems to be the position of Creation Science which requires a rewriting of science to fit into a mold of the cultural understandings of the persons who gave us Genesis, or those who have interpreted it on the basis of an earlier Western cultural heritage.

God's hand is hidden from those who bring an atheistic view to the study of science. A theistic view for the study of science discloses an astounding and growing body of information that reveals God's hidden hand in the world. This information causes us to kneel in humble reverence before the LORD God our Maker and our Savior.

God's Word and God's World Are Congruent

The scriptures of this chapter along with our interpretation of the first three chapters of Genesis help us chart the relationships we are seeking to understand in this study. We have studied God's world and word in *Genesis 1-3*, from the perspectives of theology and science. This study was intended to clarify relationships found between science and theology.

Figure 2 below shows God as the originator of what we call God's Word through deliberate revelation to speak, relate, reveal, and inspire humans in a way that their response becomes our Bible. These human responses are called formation, and are listed as speak, write, copy, select, edit, translate, and print. The Word is the divine element of Scripture, but the Bible that we can hold in our hands is the human element of Scripture. As human beings created in the divine image, we can search the biblical text. We can interpret the text, harmonize, and systematize our findings into a theology. This knowledge, without a personal relationship with God, will not show us the mystery of God. God has reached across the gulf that separates us from God through incarnation, and by becoming vulnerable in the world. We reach out to God by faith to experience God. So although God's face is hidden, and though we as created beings cannot completely comprehend God, we are given access to God's word through meditation and the illumination of Scripture that reveals God's hidden heart to us.

In a parallel way, God's action of creation is shown by the words, speak, create, form, and sustain that result in the World. Our human response to the World then results in our concept of Nature. These human responses are called sensation, and are listed as hear, see, touch, taste, smell, detect, and describe. The World is the divine element of the Cosmos, but Nature that we can describe by science is the human element of the Cosmos. As human beings created in the divine image, we can research nature. We can observe, formulate, test, and theorize our findings into a science. Again, this knowledge, without a personal relationship with God, will not show us the mystery of God's work. God has reached across the gulf that separates us from God through incarnation, and by becoming vulnerable in the world. We must reach out to God by faith to experience God. So although God's face is hidden, and as created beings we cannot completely comprehend God's creating action in the world, we are given access to God's World through contemplation and illumination of the Cosmos that reveals God's hidden hand to us.

This chart also diagrams relationships. Consideration of relationships is important in our approach to science, as related to the early

THEOLOGY and SCIENCE
A Complementary Model

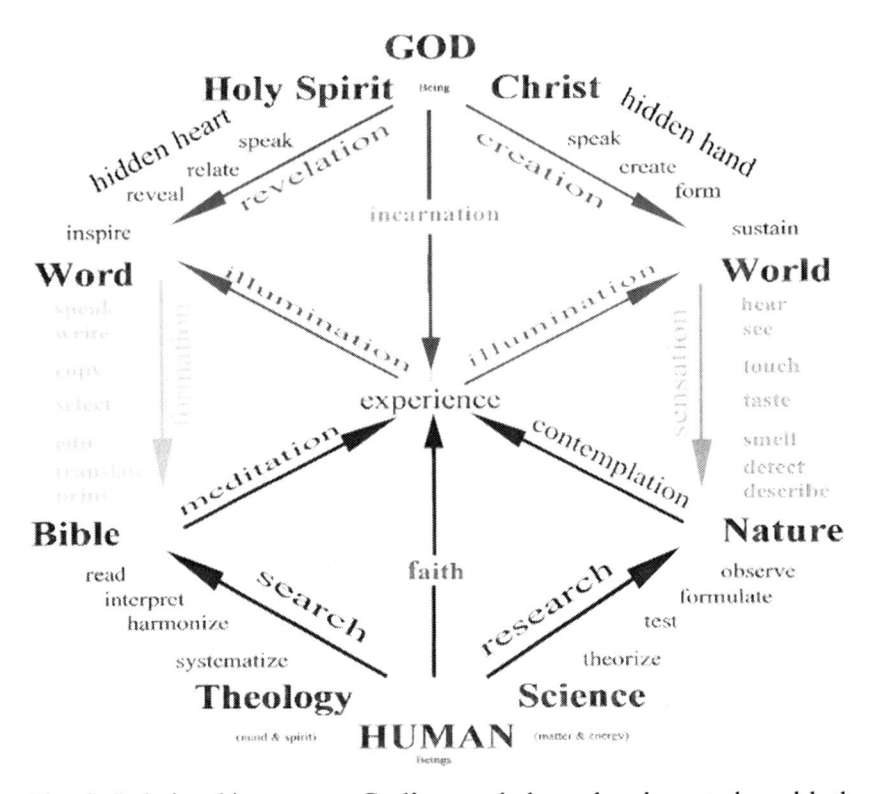

GOD
Holy Spirit — **Christ**

Word — World

Bible — Nature

Theology — **Science**
HUMAN Beings

Fig. 2. Relationships among God's revealed word and created world, the Bible and nature, theology and science, and the faith experience with God incarnate.

accounts of Genesis. Both science and theology are human activities associated with human communities, and both are subject to human limitations. In some ways they are both perspectives of the same relationship, fitting together as part of a larger whole.

Biblical theology is a study of God's Word as it is revealed in the biblical text, while science is a study of the natural World. Both the Word and the World have the same ultimate origin in God. Knowledge about the Word—theology—must come through study of God's self-revelation in the Bible. Theology needs this personal, relational element, or it becomes an academic subject easily disconnected from the truth of God.

Knowledge about the World—science—must come through study of what God has accomplished in nature. It enlarges our faith and reverence for God, when it is achieved in a committed personal relationship with God. Without such a relationship, scientific knowledge can become an element of human pride and a tool for immoral exploitation.

Human beings may not see the wholeness of Scripture and the Cosmos. God became incarnate in Christ in order to bring all things together into one. Christ is the hand, and the unity of the Christian faith experience of God in the world of matter and energy. The Holy Spirit is the heart of God, in the word of mind and spirit. It is here that we stand, not on the bases of our mastery of science or theology. The stories of the lives of persons of faith, as told in the Hebrew and Greek Bible, reflect this hand and heart of God. Faith is personal. It is trust in God, made known in personal encounter with God. Faith is a relationship to a living being, not a fixed body of knowledge about either the Word or the World. Faith can stand, even when the limited foundations of our knowledge are demolished by greater truths that lead to new comprehension.

Concluding Remarks

"*God is one*" is the affirmation of the Word of God. We experience God as the Holy Spirit in our awareness of mind and spirit. "*God is one*", but we see God as Jesus Christ incarnate in the World of matter and energy. In the realm of the Spirit, where God dwells, our emergent souls can respond to the Holy Spirit. In the realm of the material World, where we dwell, we can respond to Jesus Christ. There is only one God but we, being created in the image of God, can respond to God with our minds and our bodies. The response of Adam and Eve fell short of everything God intended in establishing a relationship with humankind. This shortfall is characteristic of all of us in our relationship to God. God's incarnate response to this shortfall, Jesus, reestablished full relationship with God for all. This is a possibility for all of us. This great drama had its beginnings in the first three chapters of Genesis.

By faith, scientific knowledge of nature, illuminated by God's Son, unveils God's hidden hand in creation of the World. The Cosmos is God's home for us.

By faith, theological knowledge of the bible, illuminated by the Holy Spirit, discloses God's hidden heart in revelation of the Word. The Scripture shows God's way for us to live in the Cosmos.

The drama begun in Genesis continues in our lives today. We are still caretakers of the earth and God's vice-regents of its creatures. By accepting the conditions of obedience for relationship with God, we reveal God's hidden heart and hand.

The purpose of Genesis is to introduce generations of humans to the God of creation and relationships. Science honors God, showing the work of His hand in every facet of creation: the material substance and the energy of the universe, as well as the functions that give it order and unity. We can rightfully be in awe of these wonderful works of God. However, it is the heart of God reaching out for relationship that moves our own heart to love and adoration. God alone is worthy of our worship, and the one who gives our own lives ultimate and eternal meaning.

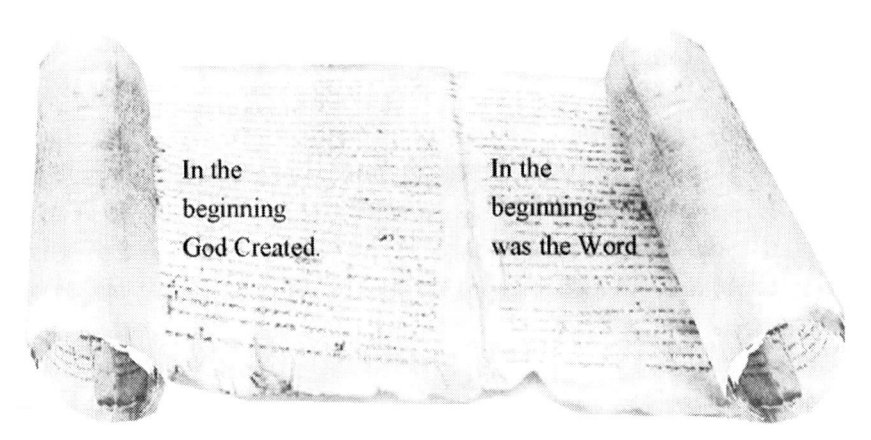

In the Beginning

Miscellaneous

Time of Creation in Science and Scriptures

Since the origin of the "Big Bang" theory of the beginning of the universe science has endeavored to set a time for the beginning of the universe. As of March 22, 2013, the current refinement of this came up with 13.77 billion years, with an uncertainty of only 0.4% for the "Big Bang" when it all got started. According to the Wikipedia article on the Age of the universe "the uncertainty of 37 million years has been obtained by the agreement of a number of scientific research projects, such as microwave background radiation measurements by the Planck satellite and other probes. Measurements of the cosmic background radiation give the cooling time of the universe since the Big Bang, and measurements of the expansion rate of the universe can be used to calculate its approximate age by extrapolating backwards in time." For many of us this has little meaning because we do not understand the theory and equations by which such calculations are made.

Age also relates to the present size of the universe since it is expanding. Stars exist in certain classes or categories related to how their nuclear furnaces function. Some always show a well known brightness and wavelength of emitted light or radiant energy. This means a dimmer appearing star is further away in the universe. By measuring brightness we can measure distance from us in years that it took a star's light to reach us. The universe must be at least as old as the time it took a star's light to reach us. Astronomers and physicists have various measuring sticks that they trust. For non-specialists it takes a measure of faith, but due to the basis of the scientific method that relies on debate, evidence, and self correction it need not be blind faith.

Although the Bible states that in the beginning God created the heaven and the earth, it does not try to give us a time for the beginning. Some will dispute this by saying that creation took place in seven days, and that from Adam on we have genealogical records in years that take us back to a beginning about 6,000 years ago. However, Genesis clearly says that the earth was without form and void and then proceeds to give functions that shape the earth with land, continents and sea, oceans with fish, heavens in which birds fly, the atmosphere as we call it and know it, and land animals including human beings. It makes sense to consider the earth in its present form a different age than the beginning of the universe, but the Bible does not tell us the amount of time between the beginning of the heaven and the beginning of the formed earth as we now know it. Science does give us this kind of a time measurement that indicates that the earth is about 4.5 billion years old or only about one third as old as the universe. There are many geologic measures for the age of different kinds of rocks mostly related to the disintegration rates of different radioactive isotopes. Geologists have put together time scales related to the layers of earth rocks and fossils that sedimentary rocks contain. So we have knowledge of how old the earth is and its changing life forms.

Psalms 90 suggests to some Bible readers that God's time is in a ratio of 1,000 years to one day of human time. But this is better seen as similar to Jesus reply whether we should forgive seven times, but Jesus said seventy times seventy. Of course Jesus did not mean count 490 times that you forgive than no longer forgive. Psalms 90 is only suggesting that the eternal God does not count time like humans count time. For me, personally, I believe like J B Phillips has suggested that "Your God Is Too Small." The God that I find in the created world as described by science gives me a greater appreciation for God's greatness and eternal nature.

In the text of this book I have suggested that we should not equate the creation of Adam and Eve with the creation of human beings in Genesis 1. Also I doubt that we can read the genealogies following the story of Adam and Eve as we would track years in genealogies that we do at present. The purpose of these genealogies was not to date the time of creation. God has not given us a scientific document for it would not make much sense over the years that the scriptures have existed. Rather God has revealed God's self that we may relate to God on a personal basis. This is a far greater truth than scientific knowledge.

Christian Hope: "In My Father's House Are Many Mansions"

If we follow Professor John Walton's understanding of the seventh day of creation as being the time for God to enter into the temple God created, then the whole universe is blessed by the presence of God. God's physical presence came to planet earth in a special way by the incarnation and birth of Jesus. Religious persons can become so spiritual that they are of no earthly good. This is not what God intends. God values the material/energy temple and earthy human beings God created as God's agents to care for our mansion in God's temple.

One of the growing and exciting areas of astronomical research is identifying other planets and planetary systems related to other stars. Discovery to date suggests that there may be billions of such systems. Unlike our past egocentric point of view that we were the center of the universe, we now know that we are not. Likely, we are not alone as intelligent beings. Certainly the Bible suggests that there are other intelligent beings. In the Bible's terminology, these other intelligent beings are called angels. Perhaps they come from other mansions, which well could be other planets.

Jesus' resurrected body had properties we cannot account for in our still limited physical sciences. He came out of the grave. Most likely, the stone was rolled away so that others could go in and know that the tomb was empty. Jesus appeared in a locked room with his still mourning disciples. How did he come through the closed doors, or did he come through the walls? He rose up into the air and disappeared into a cloud so that the disciples would understand that he had returned to heaven. Perhaps incarnation, resurrection, and ascension are God's entry into the temple of God's created universe.

Come to think of it, heaven is up from every spot on our roughly spherical earth. In other words, heaven and the heaven of all heavens are all around us. What a wonderful hope we Christians have that we will someday have bodies like Jesus' glorified body. Then we may be able to visit heaven's many mansions because we no longer have the present space-time limitations of our mortal bodies. Science is a wonderful thing, but the scriptures are even more wonderful!

Bibliography

Bible, Theology and Science

Biblesoft's New Exhaustive Strong's Numbers and Concordance with Expanded Greek-Hebrew Dictionary. Biblesoft, Inc. and International Bible Translators, Inc., 1994, 2003.

Collins, Francis S. *The Language of God*. New York, NY: Free Press, A Division of Simon & Schuster Inc., 2006.

Finger, Thomas N. *A Contemporary Anabaptist Theology: Biblical, Historical, Constructive*. Downers Grove, IL: Inter-Varsity Press, 2004

Fisher, Christopher L. "Animals, Humans and X-Men: Human Uniqueness and the Meaning of Personhood." *Theology and Science*, 3, no. 3 (2005): 291-314

Giberson, Karl W. & Francis S. Collins. *The Language of Science and Faith*. Downers Grove, IL: IVP Books, 2011.

Griffin, David Ray. *God, Power, and Evil: A Process Theodicy*. Louisville, Ky.: Westminster John Knox Press, 2004.

Griffin, David Ray. *The Two Great Truths*. Louisville, Ky.: Westminster John Knox Press, 2004

Hummel, Charles E. *Galileo Connection: Resolving Conflicts between Science & the Bible*. Downers Grove, IL: Inter-Varsity Press, 1986

Jacobs, Donald R. *What A Life!* Intercourse, PA: Good Books. 2012

Kraus, C. Norman. *Using Scripture in a Global Age*. Telford, PA. Cascadia Publishing House, 2006

McPhee, Devon. "Monkey's Morality Is Serious Business." *Science & Theology News*, 5, no. 7, (March 2005):15-17.

Miller, John W. *How the Bible Came to Be*. New York: Paulist Press, 2004

Meeks, Wayne A., General Editor. *Harper Collins Study Bible*. New York: Harper Collins Publishers, 1993

Metzger, Bruce M. and Michael D. Coogan, editors. *The Oxford Companion to the Bible*. Oxford: Oxford University Press, 1993

Moore, Andrew, *Realism and Christian Faith: God, Grammar, and Meaning*. Cambridge UK: Cambridge University Press, 2003.

Murphy, Nancey. *Reconciling Theology and Science: God, A Radical Reformation Perspective*. Scottdale, Pa.: Pandora Press, 1997

Murphy, Nancey. *Religion and Science: God, Evolution, and the Soul*. Scottdale, PA. Pandora Press, 2002

Newberg, Andrew, Eugene d'Aquili, and Vince Rouse. *Why God Won't Go Away: Brain Science and the Biology of Belief*. New York: Ballantine Books, 2001

Polkinghorne, John. *Belief in God in an Age of Science*. New Haven: Yale University Press, 1998

Redekop, Calvin, editor. *Creation & the Environment: An Anabaptist Perspective On A Sustainable World*. Baltimore: The Johns Hopkins University Press, 2000

Ruse, Michael. *Can A Darwinian Be A Christian?* Cambridge, UK: Cambridge University Press, 2001

Schroeder, Gerald L. *Genesis and the Big Bang*. New York: Bantam Books, 1990

Schroeder, Gerald L. *The Hidden Face of God*. New York: Touchstone, 2001

Schroeder, Gerald L. *The Science of God*. New York: Broadway Books, 1997

Wright, Richard T. *Biology through the Eyes of Faith*. New York: Harper & Row, 1989

Wilcox, David L. *God and Evolution: A Faith-Based Understanding*. Valley Forge, Pa.: Judson Press, 2004.

Young, Robert. *Young's Analytical Concordance to the Bible*. Peabody, MA. Hendrickson Publishers, (no date given)

History, Scientific Views and Methodologies

Barnett, S. J. *The Enlightenment and religion: The myths of modernity*. Manchester: Manchester University Press, 2003.

Behe, Michael J., William Dembski and Stephen C. Meyer. *Science and Evidence for Design in the Universe*. San Francisco: Ignatius Press, 2000

Behe, Michael J. *Darwin's Black Box*. New York: Simon & Schuster, 1996

Dawkins, Richard. *The Ancestor's Tale*. Boston: Houghton Mifflin Company, 2004

Dembski, William. *Intelligent Design*. Downers Grove, IL: Inter Varsity Press, 1999

Gould, Stephen Jay. *The Structure of Evolutionary Theory*. Cambridge, MA: The Belknap Press of Harvard University Press, 2002

Gould, Stephen Jay. *The Mismeasure of Man*. New York: W. W. Norton and Company, 1981

Knoll, Andrew H. *Life on a Young Planet: The First Three Billion Years of Evolution on Earth*. Princeton: Princeton University Press, 2003

Krauss, Lawrence M. *Atom*. Boston: Back Bay Books-Little Brown and Company, 2002

Levy, Thomas E., editor. *The Archaeology of Society in the Holy Land*. New York: Facts on File, Inc., 1995

Pinker, Stephen. *The Blank Slate*. New York: Penguin Books, 2002.

Potok, Chaim. *Wanderings*. New York: Alfred A. Knopf, 1978

Ridley, Matt. *The Agile Gene*. New York: Harper Collins Publishers Inc., 2003

Shreeve, James. "The Greatest Journey." *National Geographic*, (March 2006): 60-69

Strauss, Barry. *The Trojan War, A New History*. New York: Simon & Schuster, 2006

Genesis, Pentateuch, Old Testament

Anderson, Bernhard W. *Understanding the Old Testament*. 4th Ed. Englewood Cliffs, N.J.: Prentice-Hall, 1986

Blenkinsopp, Joseph. *The Pentateuch: An Introduction to the First Five Books of the Bible*. New York, NY: Doubleday, 1992.

Fretheim, Terence E. *The Pentateuch: Interpreting Biblical Texts*. Nashville: Abington Press, 1996

Fretheim, Terence E. "Genesis" in *The New Interpreters Bible: Vol. I, Genesis, Exodus, Leviticus*. Nashville: Abington Press, 1994.

Guengerich, Ronald. "Creation is a Continuing Event: Genesis," *Adult Bible Study Guide September, October, November 1987*. Scottdale, PA: Mennonite Publishing House, 1987

Kidner, Derek. *Genesis: An Introduction and Commentary*. Leicester, UK: Inter-Varsity Press, 1967

Mann, Thomas W. *The Book of the Torah*. Atlanta: John Knox Press, 1988

Roop, Eugene F. *Genesis: Believers Church Bible Commentary*. Scottdale, Pa.: Herald Press, 1987

Walton, John H. *The Lost World of Genesis One: Ancient Cosmology and the Origins Debate*. Downers Grove, IL: IVP Academic, 2009

Wenham, Gordon J. *Genesis 1 – 15, Word Biblical Commentary, Vol. 1*. Dallas: Word Books Publisher, 1987

Endnotes

Chapter 1 In the Beginning Was the Word

1 See page 6 of Bernhard W. Anderson, *Understanding the Old Testament*, Fourth Edition, Prentice-Hall, Englewood Cliffs, New Jersey, 1986 for a brief presentations of dates for Abraham and the Exodus from Egypt led by Moses. Other scholars may have slightly different dates, but recognize this as a long period of time.

2 Bruce M. Metzger and Michael D. Coogan, *The Oxford Companion to the Bible*, Oxford University Press, New York, 1993, p. 539.

3 Wayne A. Meeks, General Editor, *Harper Collins Study Bible*, Harper Collins Publishers, New York, 1993, p. 6.

4 Terence E. Fretheim, *The Pentateuch*, *Interpreting Biblical Texts*. Abington Press, Nashville, 1996, p. 31.

5 *Ibid*, pp. 31-32.

6 Thomas W. Mann, *The Book of the Torah*. John Knox Press, Atlanta, 1988, p. 10.

7 *Ibid*, p. 11.

8 Joseph Blenkinsopp, *The Pentateuch, An Introduction to the First Five Books of the Bible*, Doubleday, New York, 1992, p. 28.

9 Fretheim, p. 25.

10 *Ibid*, p. 26.

11 *Ibid*, p. 27.

12 *Ibid*, p. 28.

13 *Ibid*, p. 29.

14 *Ibid*.

15 Blenkinsopp, p. 42.
16 Barry Strauss, *The Trojan War, A New History*, Simon & Schuster, New York, 2006, p. xvi.
17 *Ibid.*, pp. xxi-xxii.
18 *Ibid.*, p. 185.
19 *Ibid.*, p. 3
20 Donald R. Jacobs, *What A Life*, Good Books, Intercourse, PA, 2012, p. 225.

Chapter 2 In the Beginning God Created Heaven and Earth

21 Terrence E. Fretheim, Genesis in *The New Interpreters Bible, Volume I, Genesis, Exodus, Leviticus*, Abington Press, Nashville, 1994, p. 342.
22 *Ibid.*
23 Lawrence M. Krauss, *Atom*, Back Bay Books-Little Brown and Company, Boston, 2002, pp. 27-33.
24 Gordon J. Wenham, p. 14.
25 Terrence E. Fretheim, (Genesis only), p. 342.

Chapter 3 The Functions of Time, Weather and Food Created

26 John Polkinghorne, *Belief in God in an Age of Science*, Yale University Press, New Haven, 1998, p.73
27 Gordon J. Wenham, p. 19.
28 Derek Kidner, *Genesis, An Introduction And Commentary*, Inter-Varsity Press, Leicester, England, 1967, p. 56.
29 *Ibid.*, p.58.
30 Terrence E Fretheim, (Genesis only), *The New Interpreters Bible, Volume I, Genesis, Exodus, Leviticus*, Abington Press, Nashville, 1994, p. 337.
31 Lawrence M. Krauss, pp. 164-167.
32 Lawrence M. Krauss, pp. 209-211.
33 Calvin Redekop, editor, *Creation & the Environment: An Anabaptist Perspective On A Sustainable World*, The Johns Hopkins University Press, Baltimore, 2000, p. 44.
34 Lawrence M. Krauss, pp. 158-159.
35 Andrew H. Knoll, *Life on a Young Planet; The First Three Billion Years of Evolution on Earth*, Princeton University Press, Princeton, 2003, pp. 64-65.

36 Schroeder, Gerald L., *The Science of God*, Broadway Books, New York, 1997, pp. 60-66.
37 Gordon J. Wenham, p.39
38 *Ibid.*

Chapter 4 Functionaries Installed

39 Gordon J. Wenham, p. 21.
40 Lawrence M. Krauss, pp. 152-153.
41 Stephen Jay Gould, *The Structure of Evolutionary Theory*, The Belknap Press of Harvard University Press, Cambridge, MA, 2002, p. 766 and p. 794.
42 David L. Wilcox, pp. 49-50.
43 Richard Dawkins, *The Ancestor's Tale*, Houghton Mifflin Company, Boston, 2004, pp. 248-9.

Chapter 5 Let Us Make Human Beings in Our Image

44 Terrence E Fretheim, (Genesis only), p. 345.
45 Gordon J. Wenham, pp. 27-28.
46 *Ibid.*, pp. 29-32.
47 Terrence E Fretheim, (Genesis only), p. 345.
48 Wayne A. Meeks, p7.
49 Terrence E Fretheim, (Genesis only), p. 345.
50 Terrence E Fretheim, (Genesis only), p. 346.
51 Calvin Redekop, p. 40.
52 Calvin Redekop, p. 56.
53 Calvin Redekop, p. 114.

Chapter 6 God Blessed the Seventh Day as Holy

54 Terrence E Fretheim, (Genesis only), p. 346.
55 Gordon J. Wenham, pp. 34-35.
56 Gordon J. Wenham, p. 36.
57 Terrence E Fretheim, (Genesis only), p. 346.
58 Gordon J. Wenham, p. 49.
59 Terrence E Fretheim, (Genesis only), p. 349.

Chapter 7 God, Adam and Eve in Relationship

60 *Ibid.*
61 *Ibid.*
62 Kidner, p. 44.
63 Thomas E. Levy, editor, *The Archaeology of Society in the Holy Land*, Facts on File, Inc., New York, 1995, pp. 200-201.
64 *Ibid.*, p. 226.
65 Mann, p. 17.
66 Thomas E. Levy, p. 197.
67 Ronald Guengerich, *Creation Is A Continuing Event: Genesis, Adult Bible Study Guide September, October, November 1987*, Mennonite Publishing House, Scottdale, PA, 1987, p. 5.
68 Wenham, p. 61.
69 See Stephen Jay Gould, *The Mismeasure of Man*, W. W. Norton and Company, New York, 1981.
70 See an extensive discussion of this issue in Christopher L. Fisher, "Animals, Humans and X-Men: Human Uniqueness and the Meaning of Personhood," *Theology and Science*, 3, no. 3 (2005): 291-314.
71 Kidner, p. 61.
72 *Ibid.*, p. 30.
73 James Shreeve, *The Greatest Journey*, National Geographic, March 2006, pp. 64-65.
74 Shreeve, p. 64.
75 Levy, pp. 166-167.
76 Shreeve, p. 64.
77 Chaim Potok, *Wanderings*. Alfred A. Knopf, New York, 1978, p. 5.
78 Wenham, p. 61.
79 Fretheim, Genesis, p. 350.
80 Kidner, p. 61.
81 Fretheim, Genesis, p. 351.
82 Wenham, pp. 61-2.
83 Fretheim, p. 353.
84 Wenham, p. 67.
85 Fretheim, p. 351.
86 *Ibid.*
87 Wenham, pp. 67-68.

88 Fretheim, Genesis, pp. 351-2.
89 *Ibid.*, p. 352.
90 *Ibid.*, p. 351.
91 *Ibid.*, p. 352.
92 Wenham, p. 68.
93 *Ibid.*, p. 69.
94 *Ibid.*, p. 69.
95 Fretheim, Genesis, p. 353.
96 *Ibid.*
97 Wenham, p. 69.
98 Eugene F. Roop, *Believers Church Bible Commentary, Genesis*, Herald Press, Scottdale, PA, 1987, p. 42.
99 Wenham, p. 70.
100 Fretheim, Genesis, p. 354.

Chapter 8 Adam and Eve Sin: Genesis

101 *Ibid.*, p. 359.
102 Eugene F. Roop, pp 43-44.
103 Fretheim, Genesis, pp. 359-360.
104 Robert Young, *Young's Analytical Concordance to the Bible*, Hendrickson Publishers, Peabody, MA, (no date given).
105 *Biblesoft's New Exhaustive Strong's Numbers and Concordance with Expanded Greek-Hebrew Dictionary*, 1994, 2003 Biblesoft, Inc. and International Bible Translators, Inc.
106 Wenham, pp 72-73.
107 *Ibid.*, p 57.
108 C. Norman Kraus, *Using Scripture in a Global Age*, Cascadia Publishing House, Telford PA, 2006, p 155.
109 Fretheim, Genesis, p. 360.
110 Roop, p. 44.
111 Fretheim, Genesis, p. 361.
112 *Ibid.*
113 *Ibid.*, p 361.
114 Kraus, p. 154.
115 *Ibid.*, p. 159.
116 *Ibid.*, p. 161.

Scripture and Cosmos Reconciled

117 *Ibid.*, 160-162.
118 *Ibid.*, p. 162.
119 Stephen Pinker, *The Blank Slate*, Penguin Books, New York, 2002, p. 185.
120 *Ibid.*, p. 187.
121 See chapter 9 of Thomas N. Finger, *A Contemporary Anabaptist Theology: Biblical, Historical,*
122 Wenham, p. 76.
123 *Ibid.*, p. 77
124 See discussion of morality in animals in Devon McPhee, "Monkey's Morality Is Serious Business," *Science & Theology News*, 5, no. 7, (March 2005):15-17.
125 Wenham, p. 81 and Fretheim, Genesis, p. 363.
126 Roop, pp. 45-46.
127 Wenham, p. 82.
128 Roop, pp. 46-47.
129 Wenham, p. 83.

Chapter 9 Some Perspectives

130 Fretheim, pp. 62-63.
131 Andrew Moore, *Realism and Christian Faith: God, Grammar, and Meaning*, Cambridge University Press, Cambridge UK, 2003, p. 20.
132 Moore, p. 66.
133 See these kinds of arguments in David Ray Griffin, *God, Power, and Evil; A Process Theodicy*, Westminster John Knox Press, Louisville, KY, 2004 and David Ray Griffin, *The Two Great Truths*, Westminster John Knox Press, Louisville, KY, 2004.
134 See Michael Ruse, *Can A Darwinian Be A Christian?*, Cambridge University Press, Cambridge, 2001 for arguments that a Christian can believe in a scientific view of evolution and still be a Christian.
135 Fretheim, p. 62.
136 William Dembski, *Intelligent Design*, Inter Varsity Press, Downers Grove, IL, 1999, p. 48.
137 See Michael J. Behe, William Dembski and Stephen C. Meyer, *Science and Evidence for Design in the Universe*, Ignatius Press, San Francisco, 2000 and Behe, Michael J., *Darwin's Black Box*, Simon & Schuster, New York, 1996 to understand these concepts.

138 Gordon J. Wenham, *Word Biblical Commentary*, vol. 1, Genesis 1 – 15, Word Books, Publisher, Dallas, 1987, p. 39.
139 David L. Wilcox, *God and Evolution: A Faith-Based Understanding*, Judson Press, Valley Forge, PA, 2004, p. 9.
140 Charles E. Hummel, *Galileo Connection: Resolving Conflicts between Science & the Bible*, Inter-Varsity Press, Downers Grove, IL, 1986, p. 95.
141 *Ibid.*, p. 106.

Chapter 10 Scripture and Cosmos Reconciled

142 Wenham, p. 91.
143 See arguments for the physicality of humankind yet hope of the resurrection in Nancey Murphy, *Reconciling Theology and Science: God, A Radical Reformation Perspective*, Pandora Press, Scottdale, PA., 1997 and in Nancey Murphy, *Religion and Science: God, Evolution, and the Soul*, Pandora Press, Scottdale, PA., 2002.
144 See arguments for human responsibility in Stephen Pinker, *The Blank Slate*, Penguin Books, New York, 2002 and the contribution of nurture and nature to human character in Matt Ridley, *The Agile Gene*, Harper Collins Publishers Inc., New York, 2003.
145 See neurobiological evidence for religious experience in Andrew Newberg, Eugene d'Aquili, and Vince Rouse, *Why God Won't Go Away: Brain Science and the Biology of Belief*, Ballantine Books, New York, 2001.
146 S. J. Barnett, *The Enlightenment and religion: The myths of modernity*, Manchester University Press, Manchester, 2003, p.3.

CPSIA information can be obtained at www.ICGtesting.com
Printed in the USA
BVOW03s1308180414

351034BV00004B/5/P

9 781628 715347